Mediterranean Diet Cookbook

Recipes to kick-start your Health Goals and 30 days Meal Plans.

Agatha Bellissario

This page intentionally left blank

Table of Contents

Introduzione

The Mediterranean diet might be the right solution for a heart-healthy eating plan because this diet blends the basics of healthy eating with the traditional flavors and cooking methods of the Mediterranean

However, the Mediterranean diet is not really a diet per se, as in the sense of being a weight-loss tool but it can be defined as a more of a lifestyle, or in other words, a culinary tradition for the people of the Mediterranean region. In fact, the Mediterranean diet is part of a culture that appreciates the freshest ingredients, prepared in a simple but tasty way and shared with friends and family in a laid-back environment. Additionally, this diet is also based on whole grains, fresh fruit and vegetables, seafood, nuts, olive oil, and even a glass of wine every now and then.

The Mediterranean diet was discovered in the 1960s when coronary heart disease caused fewer deaths in Mediterranean countries, such as Greece and Italy, northern Europe and later in the U.S. The main benefit of the Mediterranean diet is the highly reduced risk factors for cardiovascular disease.

The Mediterranean diet itself is based on the traditional cuisine of countries bordering the Mediterranean Sea that traditionally use high quantities of vegetables, fruits, olive oil, nuts and seeds, whole grains and beans etc. Other ingredients include daily consumption of vegetables, fruits, whole grains and healthy fats; not to mention fish, poultry, beans and eggs and a small quantity of red meat. Meals are built around these plant-based foods. The Mediterranean diet consists of great amounts of dairy, poultry and eggs. Instead, red meat is eaten only occasionally. The temperate climate and location, seasonal fresh fruit, vegetables, and seafood form the nutritional foundation of these regions may remember the food you eat during the summer.

Mediterranean diet devotees are able to enjoy their favorite dishes as they learn to appreciate how nourishing the freshest healthy and natural foods can be. For that reason the Mediterranean diet is one of the healthy eating plans recommended by the Dietary Guidelines for Americans to promote health and prevent chronic disease. The World Health Organization recognizes that the Mediterranean diet is a healthy and sustainable dietary pattern with an intangible cultural asset by the United National Educational, Scientific and Cultural Organization.

The Mediterranean diet is very helpful since you can find great pleasure in good food that provides your body with the healthiest nutrition. When your food tastes like you are on a perpetual vacation.

The particularities of the Mediterranea diet is eating more fruits and vegetables, opting for whole grains, and using healthy fats. Butter is replaced by olive oil when cooking. Instead of putting butter or margarine on bread, try dipping it in flavored olive oil.

The Mediterranean diet is a healthy and delicious way to eat. What you need to know now is how to prepare delicious recipes for you and your family. Many people who switch to this style of eating say they'll never eat any other way.

Breakfast and Brunch recipes

Breakfast Couscous

Total time: 15 minutes

 Prep time: 10 minutes

Cook time: 5 minutes

Yield: 4 servings

Ingredients:

1or 2 inch cinnamon stick

3 cups 1% low-fat milk

1 cup whole-wheat couscous (uncooked)

6 tablespoons of dark brown sugar, divided

¼ cup dried currants

½ cup chopped apricots

 ¼ tablespoon of sea salt

4 tablespoons of melted butter, divided

Directions:

First take a saucepan and put cinnamon sticks and milk and set over medium high heat for about 3 or 5 minutes paying attention not to boil it. After that, remove the pan from heat and stir in couscous, 4 teaspoons of sugar, currants, apricots, and sea salt. Let the mixture stand, covered, for at least 15 or 20 minutes. Then discard the cinnamon stick and divide the couscous among four bowls; top each serving with ½ teaspoon of sugar and 1 teaspoon of melted butter. Serve hot and enjoy your breakfast

Black beans bowl

Total time: 40 minutes

 Prep time: 5 minutes

Cook time: 35 minutes

Yield: 4 servings

Ingredients:

2 tablespoons of olive oil

4 beaten eggs

15 ounce of drained and rinsed can black beans

1 avocado, peeled and sliced

¼ cup salsa

Salt and ground black pepper

Directions:

Take a small pan and heat olive oil over medium heat. Cook and stir eggs for a few minutes (3 to 5 minutes) until they are set. Place black beans in a microwave-safe bowl. After that heat on high in the microwave until warm, it will not take more than 1 minute. Divide warmed black beans between two bowls and top each bowl with the mixture of eggs, avocado, and salsa. Season with salt and black pepper or with whatever you like. Serve and eat immediately.

Steel-cut Oats Breakfast

Total time: 30 minutes

Prep time: 5 minutes

Cook time: 25 minutes

Yield: 4 servings

Ingredients:

Some cups of water

½ cup quinoa

½ cup steel-cut oats

2 tablespoons of almond meal and 2 of flaxseed meal

1 tablespoon ground cinnamon

Directions:

Take a saucepan and bring water to a boil after that add quinoa and oats. Simmer, stirring continuously in order to make the water absorbed. It will take about 20 minutes for quinoa to become tender. After that, stir almond meal and flaxseed meal into quinoa mixture; pour into a glass container and top with cinnamon. Let it cool (more or less for 15 minutes). Transfer to the refrigerator. Serve whenever you want.

Fruity Nutty Muesli

Total time: 1 hour 15 minutes

Prep time 15 minutes

 Cook time 1 hour

Yield: 2 servings

Ingredients:

⅓ cup of chopped almonds

¾ cup of toasted oats

½ cup low-fat milk

½ cup low-fat Greek yogurt

½ green apple

2 tablespoon of raw honey

Directions:

Start preheating the oven to 350°F. Bake the almonds on a baking sheet until they turn golden brown. It will probably take about 10 minutes. After cooling, mix with the toasted oats, milk and yogurt in a bowl and cover. Refrigerate this mixture for at least an hour to make the oats soft. Before serving, divide the muesli between two bowls, add the apple and drizzle the honey.

Potato and Chickpea Hash

Total time: 15 minutes

Prep time: 10 minutes

Cook time: 5 minutes

Yield: 4 servings

Ingredients:

4 cups of hash brown potatoes

2 cups chopped baby spinach

1 tablespoon of minced ginger

½ cup chopped onion

1 tablespoon curry powder

½ tablespoon of sea salt

¼ cup extra virgin olive oil

1 cup chopped zucchini

15-ounce of rinsed chickpeas

4 large eggs

Directions:

Combine the potatoes, ginger, onion, spinach, curry powder, and sea salt in a large bowl. After that add this potato mixture in a nonstick skillet and set over medium high heat, don't forget to add extra virgin olive oil. Keep pressing the mixture into a layer and cook at the same temperature for about 6 minutes, without stirring. When it becomes golden brown and crispy it means it is ready. At this point, lower heat to medium low and fold in zucchini and chickpeas, breaking up the mixture until just combined. Stir briefly, press the mixture back into a layer, and make four wells. Break one egg into each indentation. Then cook, and keep it covered for about 5 minutes in order to set the eggs.

Mushroom Wonton

Total time: 25 minutes

Prep time: 10 minutes

Cook time: 20 minutes

Yield: 4 servings

Ingredients for dough:

1 ½ cup all-purpose flour

½ tsp. salt or to taste

Water

Ingredients for filling:

2 cups cubed mushroom

2 tablespoons of oil

2 tablespoons of ginger-garlic paste

2 tsp. soya sauce

2 tsp. vinegar

Directions:

Start kneading the dough. Once you cover it with plastic wrap and set aside. After that, cook the ingredients for the filling making sure that the mushrooms are completely covered with the sauce. At this point, roll the dough and place the filling in the center. Preheat your oven at 200° F for 5 minutes (eventually you can use an airfryer). While waiting wrap the dough to cover the filling and pinch the edges together. Transfer the dumplings in the oven and cook them at the same temperature for about 20 minutes.

Mediterranean Scones

Total time: 30 minutes

Prep time: 15 minutes

Cook time: 15 minutes

Yield: 12 servings

Ingredients:

2 cups plus ¼ cup flour

½ tablespoon of baking soda

2 tablespoons of sugar

½tablespoon of sea salt

¾ cup reduced-fat buttermilk

Zest of 1 lemon

1 to 2 tablespoons of squeezed lemon juice

1 cup powdered sugar

Directions:

Preheat your oven to 400°F. In the meanwhile, put in a food processor 2 cups of flour, baking soda, sugar and salt and mix together until it becomes well blended. Combine buttermilk and lemon zest and keep mixing to blend properly. Sprinkle the remaining flour onto a clean surface and turn out the dough; gently knead the dough at least six times and shape it into a ball. I suggest using a rolling pin, so you can flatten the dough into a half-inch thick circle. After cutting the dough into four equal wedges, go ahead and cut each into three smaller wedges. Arrange the scones on a baking sheet and bake in a preheated oven for about 15 minutes or just the time it will be golden brown. Combine together lemon juice and the powdered sugar in a small bowl to make a thin frosting. Remove the scones from the oven and drizzle with lemon frosting while still hot. Serve right away and enjoy.

Mediterranean Wrap

Total time: 10 minutes

Prep time: 5 minutes

Cooking time: 5 minutes

Yield: 2 servings

Ingredients:

½ cup fresh-picked spinach

4 egg whites

2 sun-dried tomatoes

2 mixed-grain flax wraps

½ cup feta cheese crumbles

Directions:

Start combining spinach, egg whites with tomatoes in a frying pan and cook it for about 5 minutes until lightly browned. Then flip it over and cook the other side for 5 minutes or even less. You can then microwave the wraps for a few seconds; after removing from the microwave, fill each wrap with the egg mixture, sprinkle with feta cheese crumbles and roll up. Cut each wrap into two parts and serve hot.

Clams galette

Total time: 30 minutes

Prep time: 5 minutes

Cooking time: 25 minutes

Ingredients:

2 tablespoons of garam masala

1-2 tablespoons of. fresh coriander leaves

Salt and pepper to taste

1 lb. minced clam

3 tablespoons of ginger finely chopped

2 or 3 green chilies finely chopped

1 ½ tablespoons of lemon juice

Directions:

Combine together all the ingredients in a clean bowl. After molding this mixture into round and flat galettes, you have to wet the galettes with water. Preheat your oven at 160 degrees Fahrenheit for 5 minutes. Transfer the galettes there to cook for another 25 minutes or more at the same temperature. Continue rolling them over to get a uniform result. Serve warm.

Yogurt Pancakes

Total time: 15 minutes

Prep time: 10 minutes

Cooking time: 5 minutes

Yield: 5 servings

Ingredients:

Whole-wheat pancake mix

1 cup yogurt 1 tablespoon of baking powder

1 tablespoon of baking soda

1 cup skimmed milk

3 whole eggs

½ tablespoon of extra virgin olive oil

Directions:

Take a large bowl to combine together the whole-wheat pancake mix with yogurt, baking powder, baking soda, skimmed milk and eggs;and then stir until well blended. Therefore, heat a pan oiled lightly with olive oil and pour the batter onto the heated pan and cook for 1 or at least 2 minutes until you can see some bubbles on the surface of your pancakes. Next, flip and continue cooking until the underside is browned. Serve the pancakes warm with a cup of fat-free milk or two tablespoons of light maple syrup and enjoy your breakfast.

Quiche Wrapped

Total time: 25 minutes

Prep time: 10 minutes

Cook time: 15 minutes

Yield: 8 servings

Ingredients:

4 halved slices of prosciutto

2 egg whites

1 egg

½ tablespoon of fresh and chopped rosemary

3 tablespoons of low fat Greek yoghurt

1 tablespoon of chopped black olives

A pinch of black pepper, freshly ground

A pinch of salt

Directions:

First preheat your oven to 400°F and coat your muffin baking tray with cooking spray. Put each prosciutto piece into eight cups of the tray and cook in a medium bowl, without forgetting to whisk the egg whites and the egg until smooth. Keep whisking and later add yogurt, rosemary, olives, pepper, and salt. Divide the mixture equally among the prosciutto cups and bake uncovered until cooked through (not more than 20 minutes). Garnish with rosemary and enjoy your meal.

Feta and Greek Yogurt

Total time: 10 minutes

Prep time: 10 minutes

Cook time: 0 minutes

Yields: 8 servings

Ingredients:

¼ cup crumbled tomato-basil feta cheese

2 tablespoons of reduced-fat mayonnaise

1 container of Greek fat-free plain yogurt

2 tablespoon of fresh parsley, chopped

Assorted fresh vegetables

Directions:

Combine cheese, mayonnaise, with yogurt and parsley in a small bowl until well blended, then divide the dip among bowls and serve with your favorite vegetables.

Ham and eggs

Total time: 25 minutes

Prep time: 5 minutes

Cook time: 20 minutes

Yield: 4 servings

Ingredients:

Bread slices (brown or white)

½ lb. sliced ham

1 egg white

A pinch of sugar

Directions:

Preheat your oven or your airfryer at 180° C for 4 minutes. In the meanwhile put two slices together and cut them along the diagonal. Whisk the egg whites and in a bowl and apply some sugar. After that, dip the bread triangles into this mixture. After that, cook the ham at the same temperature said before for another 20 minutes or more. Don't forget that halfway through the process, you have to turn the triangles over in order to get a uniform cook. Top with ham and serve hot.

Mediterranean Seafood

Italian-style fish with olives and capers

Total time: 21 minutes

Prep time: 5 minutes

Cook time: 16 minutes

Yield: 4 servings

Ingredients:

4 tablespoons of extra virgin olive oil

5 ounce of sea bass fillets

1 diced small onion

1 cup canned diced tomatoes, with juice

½ cup pitted black olives, chopped

½ cup white wine

2 tablespoons of capers

2 cups fresh baby spinach leaves

¼ tablespoon of crushed red pepper

Sea salt and pepper

Directions:

Heat 2 teaspoons of extra virgin olive oil in a large skillet set over low or medium high heat and add fish. In this way, cook for about 5 minutes per side until it turns opaque in the center. Doing so, transfer the cooked fish to a plate and keep it warm. Sauté onion for about 5 minutes until translucent and combine the remaining oil to the skillet. Stir in wine and cook for about 4 minutes or until liquid is reduced. At this point, stir in capers, tomatoes, olives, and red pepper and cook for another 3 or 4 minutes. After adding spinach and cooking, stirring until silted (for about 4 minutes). Stir in sea salt and pepper and spoon sauce over fish. Serve immediately and enjoy it.

Pasta with shrimp

Total time: 20 minutes

Prep time: 15 minutes

Cook time: 5 minutes

Yield: 4 servings

Ingredients:

2 tablespoons of drained capers

2 tsp. extra virgin olive oil

2 minced of garlic cloves

4 cups hot cooked angel hair pasta

¼ cup crumbled feta cheese

Cooking spray

1 peeled pound shrimp

2 cups of chopped plum tomato

¼ cup thinly sliced fresh basil

⅓ cup chopped pitted Kalamata olives

¼ tablespoons of freshly ground black pepper

Directions:

Take a large nonstick skillet and heat 2 tablespoons of extra virgin olive oil and add up garlic and sauté for about a few seconds. After mixing together shrimp go ahead and sauté for 1 minute or even more. Mix up the tomato and basil and lower heat to medium low; simmer until the tomato is tender for about 3 minutes. After that, stir in capers, black pepper as well as Kalamata olives. At the end, in a large bowl, put the shrimp mixture in the pasta and toss to mix and top with cheese. Serve warm and eat immediately.

Mediterranean Flounder

Total time: 40 minutes

Prep time: 10 minutes

Cook time: 30 minutes

Yield: 4 servings

Ingredients:

5 Italians tomatoes

2 tablespoons of extra virgin olive oil

½ chopped onion

2 chopped garlic cloves

1 pinch Italian seasoning

1 lb. flounder/tilapia/halibut

4 tablespoons of capers

24 Kalamata olives, pitted and chopped

1 tablespoons of freshly lemon juice, squeezed

¼ cup white wine

6 leaves fresh basil, chopped; divided

3 tablespoons of Parmesan cheese

Directions:

Preheat your oven to 425⁰F and then plunge the tomatoes into boiling water and peel the skins and chop them before transferring them into a bowl of ice water. Proceed adding extra virgin olive oil to a skillet set over medium heat and sauté onions until they turn translucent. Mix tomatoes, garlic, Italian seasoning, and cook everything until tomatoes are tender. Stir lemon juice, capers,olives, and half of basil in wine. Lower heat and stir in Parmesan cheese and after that cook for about 15 minutes until the mixture is bubbly and quite hot. Next, place fish in a baking dish and cover with the sauce; at the end bake in the preheated oven until fish is cooked through (for about 20 minutes).

Mediterranean Halibut

Total time: 30 minutes

Prep time: 5 minutes

Cook time: 25minutes

Yield: 4 servings

Ingredients:

2 bell peppers

2 cups grape tomatoes

2 cans artichoke hearts

1 cup pitted kalamata olives

1 teaspoon dried oregano

4 fillets wild halibut

kosher salt (for the fish)

freshly ground black pepper

1 teaspoon of dried oregano

1/2 teaspoon of garlic powder

kosher salt

1/2 teaspoon garlic powder

1/2 teaspoon red pepper flakes

1/2 teaspoon of red pepper flakes

fresh flat leaf parsley (optional)

Directions:

Strain the artichokes and olives and transfer to a mixing bowl. After that, preheat the oven to 375°F. You should then remove the cores and stems from the bell peppers and cut into 1/ 4 or 1/5-inch-wide strips. Transfer the peppers to the bowl, add the tomatoes with the artichokes and olives. Arrange a sheet pan with parchment paper where you will put the contents of the bowl to the prepared pan on. Next, season with kosher salt, the oregano, garlic powder, and red pepper flakes. Cook for at least 10 minutes in the oven until olives start to shrivel and tomatoes begin to blister. Season the fish on parchment paper again with salt, pepper. After removing the vegetables from the oven. cover the fish with the vegetables. Return to the oven and cook again (for 10/15minutes) making sure that the fish is cooked through. Once the fish is well cooked, remove it from the oven and transfer it to serving plates, trying to divide the vegetables between each serving. I recommend you to sprinkle a little over each serving for garnish, serve and enjoy.

Light Salmon Bean

Total time: 20 minutes

Prep time: 10 minutes

Cook time: 10 minutes

Yield: 4 servings

Ingredients:

1g of crushed red pepper

2.5g cornstarch 5ml rice wine

7.5ml black bean-garlic sauce

7.5ml rice vinegar

30ml cup water

5ml canola oil

100g salmon, skinned, cubed 10g scallions, sliced 90g bean sprouts

Directions:

Whisk together cornstarch, crushed red pepper, rice wine, bean garlic sauce, vinegar in a bowl,and add water in order to combine well. Heat oil over medium heat, and stir in fish and cook for about 1 or 2 minutes. Combine together scallions and sprout in the sauce mixture. Cook for about 4 minutes until the sprouts are tender and cooked down. Serve and enjoy it!

Tuna Sandwich

Total time: 21 minutes

Prep time: 5 minutes

Cook time: 16 minutes

Yield: 2 servings

Ingredients:

2 slices of white bread

1 tablespoon of softened butter

1 tin tuna

1 small capsicum

Ingredients For the Sauce:

1 lb ripe tomatoes, seeded and coarsely chopped

½ teaspoon dried thyme

½ teaspoon dried basil

Olive oil and salt and pepper

1 teaspoon of chopped fresh chives

½ teaspoon dried oregano

2 green onions or 2 scallions, finely chopped

⅓ cup of dry white vermouth

lbs fish fillets (as you wish)

Butter (optional)

Directions:

Remove the slices of bread and cut each slice horizontally. Cook the ingredients for the sauce and until the composure thickens. At this point, combine the lamb to the sauce and mix everything until you obtain the flavors. At this point, roast the capsicum peeling the skin off. Make sure of cutting the capsicum into slices. After mixing together all the ingredients, apply it to the bread slices. Preheat the oven at 300 Fahrenheit and cook both sides. After that, turn down the heat for another 15 minutes. Don't forget to turn each sandwich in between during the cooking process to cook both slices perfectly. Serve the sandwiches and enjoy your meal!

Grilled Salmon

Total time: 23 minutes

Prep time: 15 minutes

Cook time: 8 minutes

Yield: 4 servings

Ingredients:

2 tablespoons of freshly squeezed lemon juice

1 tablespoons of minced garlic

1 tablespoons of chopped fresh parsley

4 tablespoons of chopped fresh basil

4 salmon fillets

Extra virgin olive oil

Sea salt as much as necessary

Cracked black pepper, to taste

4 chopped green olives

Cracked black pepper

4 thin slices lemon

Directions:

Lightly coat grill rack with olive oil cooking spray; heat grill to medium high. Mix together lemon juice, minced garlic, parsley and basil in a small bowl. After doing that apply extra virgin olive oil to the fish and season it with sea salt and pepper. Prepare a herb-side grill where you will place each fish fillet topped with an equal amount of garlic mixture. Grill the fish over high heat for about 4 or 5 minutes until the edges turn white; turn over and transfer the fish to aluminum foil. Turn down the heat and continue grilling for another 4 or 5 minutes. At the end, transfer the grilled fish to plates and garnish with lemon slices and green olives. Serve immediately and eat warm.

Baked mackerel with lemon

Total time: 35 minutes

Prep time: 10 minutes

Cook time: 25 minutes

Yield: 4 servings

Ingredients:

3 tablespoons of extra-virgin olive oil

1 red bell pepper, stemmed, seeded, and chopped fine

1 chopped red onion

½ preserved lemon, pulp and white pith removed

⅓ chopped cup pitted brine-cured green olives

1 tablespoon of minced fresh parsley

Salt and pepper

10-ounce of snipped mackerel

Directions:

First heat oil in a 12-inch skillet over lower or medium high heat until shimmering. Combine pepper and onion and cook until vegetables are softened and well browned (at least for 9-10 minutes). Stir in preserved lemon and keep cooking so that it will be fragrant. Remove from the heat, mix together olives and parsley and season with salt and pepper, just a bit. After that, grease rimmed the baking sheet with oil. It's important to wash each mackerel carefully under cold running water. After opening the cavity of each mackerel, you have to season the flesh with salt and pepper, and spoon one quarter of filling into the opening. Transfer mackerel on a prepared sheet in a way that each piece is well separated. Bake 130 to 135 degrees for 15 minutes. until thick. Carefully transfer the mackerel to a serving platter and let rest for 5 minutes before eating. It's good to serve baked mackerel with lemon wedges.

Salmon and Vegetable Kedgeree

Total time: 30 minutes

Prep time: 10 minutes

Cook time: 20 minutes

Ingredients:

60ml basmati rice

7.5ml extra virgin olive oil

2g curry powder

100g skinless flaked hot-smoked salmon portions

100g vegetable mix Sea salt and pepper, to taste

1 green onion, thinly sliced

Directions:

Take a saucepan and boil water, add salt and the rice, turn heat to low and cook, covered, until just tender, for about 12 minutes or more. Combine extra virgin olive oil to a pan set over medium heat and cook the onion, stirring until tender, for about 5 minutes. Stir in curry powder and keep cooking until fragrant, for 2 minute. Stir in rice until well combined and then add salmon, vegetables, salt and pepper. Keep cooking until heated through, for about a few minutes before serving.

Delicious fish club sandwich

Total time: 30 minutes

Prep time: 10 minutes

Cook time: 20 minutes

Ingredients:

2 slices of white bread

1 tablespoon of softened butter

1 tin tuna

1 small capsicum

Ingredients for Delicate Sauce:

½ tablespoon of olive oil

½ crushed flake garlic

¼ cup chopped onion

¼ tablespoon of mustard powder

½ tablespoon of sugar

¼ tablespoon of red chili sauce

1 tablespoon of tomato ketchup

Water

A pinch of salt and black pepper to taste

Directions:

Remove the slices of bread and remove the edges and cut each slice horizontally. After that, cook the ingredients mentioned above for the sauce until the mix thickens. At this point, combine the fish to the sauce and stir till it obtains the flavors. After roasting the capsicum and peeling the skin off, try to cut the capsicum into slices. Combine the ingredients and apply it to the bread slices. Use your air fryer or oven to cook, making sure to preheat it for 5 minutes at 200 Fahrenheit before starting to turn down the heat at 180 degrees for around 15 minutes. In order to cook both slices, you should turn the sandwiches in between during the cooking process. Serving the sandwiches with another home-made sauce could also be a good idea.

Roasted Fish

Total time: 40 minutes

Prep time: 10 minutes

Cook time: 30 minutes

Yields: 4 servings

Ingredients:

1 tablespoon of olive oil

A pinch ground pepper

1 (14-oz) can drained artichoke hearts

1 tablespoons of fennel seed

1 ½ lb. quartered of cod

4 ½ tablespoons of grated orange peel

4 crushed of cloves garlic

1 green bell pepper, cut into small strips

½ cup halved pitted olives

1 pint cherry tomatoes

2 tablespoons of drained capers

⅓ cup fresh orange juice

A pinch salt

Directions:

Firstly, preheat your oven to 450°F. Grease a medium-size piece or cut it in half of a baking pan with 1 tablespoon olive oil. Arrange the artichoke hearts, bell pepper, olives, tomatoes, garlic, and fennel seed in the prepared pan. Transfer the fish over the vegetables and top with orange peel, capers, orange juice, pepper and salt everything.

Mediterranean Cod

Total time: 50 minutes

Prep time: 15 minutes

Cook time: 35 minutes

Yield: 4 servings

Ingredients:

1 tablespoon of extra virgin olive oil

230g can Italian tomatoes, chopped

1 tablespoon of tomato purée

400g pack skinless and boneless cod fillets

100g frozen chopped onion

1 tablespoon of frozen chopped garlic

50g pitted black olives

1 tablespoons of chopped frozen parsley

200g frozen mixed peppers

800g package frozen white rice

Directions:

Heat extra virgin olive oil to a saucepan set over medium heat; stir in onion and sauté for about 4 minutes. Apply garlic and sauté until fragrant. Combine together the tomatoes, tomato puree, and water and bring to boil. At this point, reduce heat and simmer for about 20 minutes until it becomes thickened. Season with cod and peppers; after that nudge the fish in the sauce a bit and bring back to a boil; lower heat again and simmer. Season with parsley and olives and simmer for a few minutes. While waiting, follow package instructions and cook rice. Adding fish on top of hot rice and enjoy it.

Marinated Artichokes

Total time: 45 minutes

Prep time: 10 minutes

Cook time: 35 minutes

Yield: 6 to 8 servings

Ingredients:

4 pounds baby artichokes

8 peeled of garlic cloves

2 tablespoons of minced fresh mint

2 lemons

6 smashed cloves

2½ cups extra-virgin olive oil

¼ teaspoon red pepper flakes

2 minced cloves

2 sprigs fresh thyme

Salt and pepper as much as necessary

Directions:

Firstly, remove lemon zest with a vegetable peeler and grate ½ teaspoon zest from the second lemon and set aside. Halve and juice lemons to yield. Mix up oil and lemon zest strips in a large saucepan. Taking 1 artichoke at a time, cut the top quarter off each artichoke, snap off outer leaves, and remove their dark parts. After peeling and trimming the stem, cut artichoke in half lengthwise. Try to rub each artichoke half with spent lemon half and place in a saucepan. Combine together smashed garlic, pepper flakes, thyme sprigs, pepper and salt to saucepan and bring to rapid simmer over high heat. Turn the heat to medium-low and simmer, stirring sometimes just to submerge all artichokes. Try to pierce artichokes with a fork to be sure they are still firm. Take off the heat, cover it , and let sit until artichokes are fully cooked (fork-tender). It will take probably 20 minutes. Stir gently in ½ teaspoon reserved grated lemon zest, and ¼ cup reserved lemon juice, and minced garlic. Place artichokes and oil to a serving bowl and let it cool to room temperature before seasoning with a pinch of salt. Sprinkle with mint and serve.

Vegetarian Mediterranean Recipes

Delicious Swiss Chard

Total time: 20 minutes

Prep time: 5 minutes

Cook time: 10 minutes

Yield: 2 servings

Ingredients:

2 garlic cloves, sliced

1 sliced of small yellow onion

Kalamata olives 1 chopped of jalapeno pepper

⅓ pitted and roughly chopped of cup

1 tablespoon of extra virgin olive oil

Water as much as necessary

1 ¼ pounds trimmed and rinsed Swiss chard

Directions:

Separate stems from leaves of Swiss chard in order to cut the stems into small pieces and chop roughly the leaves. After that, heat extra virgin olive oil in a large skillet over medium heat or using an oven. Combine together garlic, onion, and jalapeno; sauté for a few minutes until you see that the onion is tender and translucent. Mix together with olives, Swiss chard stems, water and cook again making sure to cover it for the following 3 minutes. Stir in the chard leaves and keep covered cooking for about 4 or 5 minutes. When the leaves and stems are tender, it's time to serve and enjoy it!

Italian Salad

Total time: 20 minutes

Prep time: 5 minutes

Cook time: 15 minutes

Yield: 4 servings

Ingredients:

½ head cauliflower cut into small inch florets

3 peeled and sliced carrots

3 celery ribs, cut crosswise into small pieces

2¾ cups white wine vinegar

¼ inch thick on bias

1 cup chopped fresh dill

1 red bell pepper cut finely

2 sliced thin serrano chiles

4 sliced thin of garlic cloves

¼ cup sugar

Water as much as you need

2 tablespoons of salt

Directions:

Combine in a large bowl cauliflower, celery, carrots, with garlic, bell pepper and serranos. At this point, transferring everything into small jars with tight-fitting lids would be better. Bundle dill in cheesecloth and combine together with kitchen twine to secure. Bring dill sachet, and other ingredients to boil in a large saucepan over medium-high heat. After removing from heat, steep it for 15 minutes and now discard dill sachet and return brine to a brief boil, then pour evenly over vegetables. Let cool to room temperature covered with a kitchen towel, then refrigerate it until vegetables taste pickled, at least 7 days or more.

Yummy Vegetable Patties

Total time: 20 minutes

Prep time: 5 minutes

Cook time: 15 minutes

Yield: 2 servings

Ingredients:

¼ tsp. cumin powder

1 cup grated mixed vegetables

A pinch of salt to taste

¼ tsp. ginger finely chopped

1 tbsp. fresh coriander leaves

¼ tsp. red chili powder

1 green chili finely chopped

1 tsp. lemon juice

Directions:

Combine all the ingredients together making sure that the flavors are right. At this point, you should make round patties with the mixture and roll them out gently.

Preheat the oven at 250 Fahrenheit for 5 minutes and then arrange the patties to cook at 150 degrees for around 10 or 12 minutes. In between the cooking process, don't forget to turn the patties over to obtain a uniform cook. Serve hot with your favorite home-made sauce or salad.

Grilled Veggies Tagine

Total time: 1 hour

Prep time: 10 minutes

Cook time: 50 minutes

Yield: 6 servings

Ingredients:

¼ cup golden raisins

6 small cut red potatoes

¼ toasted cup pine nuts

2/3 uncooked cup couscous

2 garlic cloves, pressed

Wedged red onion

1 tablespoon of crushed fennel seeds

¼ tablespoon of ground cinnamon

1 ¾ chopped cups onions

1 tablespoon of extra virgin olive oil

1 tablespoon of ground cumin

¼ cup green olives, pitted and chopped

Water

¼ tablespoon of freshly ground black pepper

Cooking spray

2 diced red bell peppers,

1 diced green bell pepper

½ tablespoon of kosher salt

2 tablespoons of balsamic vinegar

½ can tomatoes

Directions:

Start preparing a gas or charcoal grill and then combine together in a zip lock plastic bag the bell peppers, a teaspoon of sea salt, red onion, and vinegar and a teaspoon olive oil and toss well. Place a large nonstick saucepan on medium heat and mix the remaining olive oil as well as the garlic and the chopped onion before sauté these for about 5 minutes and combine fennel, cumin with cinnamon. After 1 or 2 minutes of cooking, water the remaining raisins, salt, olives, tomatoes, potatoes, black pepper and bring the pan to a boil. Simmer for 25 minutes covering the saucepan. When the potatoes are tender, you should remove the onions and bell peppers from the plastic bag and grill on a rack coated with cooking spray for about 10 minutes. After that, boil the remaining water in a separate saucepan and stir slowly in the couscous. Turn down the heat and cover the pan and let it stand for another 5 minutes. Place the tomato mixture on the couscous and top with the grilled onions, bell peppers and pine nuts before serving.

Aloo Patties

Total time: 20 minutes

Prep time: 5 minutes

Cook time: 15 minutes

Yield: 2 servings

Ingredients:

1 cup mashed potato

A pinch of salt to taste

¼ tablespoons of chopped finely ginger

1 green chili finely chopped

1 tablespoon of lemon juice

1 tablespoon of fresh coriander leaves

¼ tablespoons of red chili powder

¼ tablespoons of cumin powder

Directions:

Combine together all the ingredients making sure that flavors are well balanced. Using your hands, make round patties with the mixture and roll them out gently. Preheat your oven or in case your air fryer at 250 Fahrenheit for a few minutes. Turn down the heat at around 150 degrees for around 15 minutes turning the patties over to get a uniform cook during the entire process of cooking. Serve immediately and enjoy it!

Zucchini Sauté and Green Bean

Total time: 15 minutes

Prep time: 5 minutes

Cook time: 10 minutes

Yield: 4 servings

Ingredients:

7.5 ml lemon juice

7.5 ml divided olive oil

50g trimmed green beans cut into small pieces

15g sliced scallions

½ thinly sliced small zucchini

2g red chili flakes

Handful of parmesan flakes

1g red chili flakes

Salt and pepper

Directions:

Heat oil to a skillet set over medium heat. Combine together green beans, zucchini, salt and pepper and sauté, mixing up for about 10 minutes until you see that the vegetables are crisp tender. Transfer the pan from heat and add lemon juice, scallions. Garnished with red chili flakes and cheese and serve.

Spinach Cake

Total time: 1 hour

Prep time: 15 minutes

Cook time: 45 minutes

Yields: 12 Spinach Cakes

Ingredients:

1 ½ rinsed pounds spinach

3 tablespoons of extra virgin olive oil

½ cup currants

1 tablespoon of sea salt

2 whisked of large eggs

2 minced of cloves garlic

1 cup pine nuts

Directions:

First, wilt spinach in a pan set over low heat for about 6 minutes; drain and let cool at room temperature for 10 minutes before squeezing moisture out of the spinach. After that, pulse the spinach in a food processor until they are chopped. Warm oil in a skillet and combine pine nuts and sauté for a few minutes until golden brown. Combine together garlic and keep cooking for a few minutes. After adding the currants, blended spinach, eggs and the pine nut mixture, salt in a bowl; finally spread the mixture into a coated baking dish and bake at 350°F for about 35 minutes.

Yam galette

Total time: 35 minutes

Prep time: 10 minutes

Cook time: 25 minutes

Yield: 6 servings

Ingredients:

2 cups minced yam

3 tablespoons of chopped finely ginger

2 or 3 chopped green chilies finely

1 ½ tablespoons of lemon juice

1-2 tablespoons of fresh coriander leaves

Salt and pepper to taste

Directions:

Preheat your oven (or air fryer eventually) at 160 degrees Fahrenheit for about 5 minutes. In the meanwhile, combine together the ingredients in a clean bowl, and mold this mixture into round and flat galettes. Proceed wetting the galettes slightly with water. Transfer the galettes in the oven and let them cook at the same temperature for another 25 minutes. Continue rolling them over to get a uniform cook on both sides. Serve hot and enjoy it!

Cottage cheese Gnocchi

Total time: 45 minutes

Prep time: 10 minutes

Cook time: 35 minutes

Yield: 2 servings

Ingredients for dough:

1 ½ cup all-purpose flour

2 cups crumbled cottage cheese

2 tablespoons of oil

½ tablespoon of salt

Water

Ingredients for filling:

2 tablespoons of ginger-garlic paste

2 tablespoons of vinegar

2 tablespoons of soya sauce

Directions:

First at all, knead the dough and then cover it with plastic wrap and set aside. After that, cook the ingredients for the filling making sure that the cottage cheese is totally covered with the sauce. After rolling the dough cut it into a square, anche transfer the filling in the center wrapping the dough in order to cover the filling and pinch the edges together. Before or after that, preheat your air fryer or oven at 200° F for 6 minutes. Transfer in the oven and cook at the same temperature for another 25 minutes. You can serve with a lot of vegetables.

Chickpea Salad

Total time: 1 hour, 20 minutes

Prep time: 10 minutes

Cook time: 40 minutes

Standing time: 30 minutes

Yield: 6 servings

Ingredients:

3tablespoon of sherry vinegar

16 crushed whole black peppercorns

¾ tablespoon of dried oregano

3 scallions, sliced into small pieces

2 diced carrots

1 ½ cups dried chickpeas, soaked and liquid reserved

1 ¼ tablespoon of divided sea salt

1 minced of garlic clove

½ diced cucumber

2 cups halved cherry tomatoes

 2 tablespoon of extra virgin olive oil

1 cup diced green bell pepper

3 tablespoon of chopped fresh parsley

2 tablespoons of shredded fresh basil

Directions:

Firstly combine together the chickpeas and soaking liquid in a large pot and season with a teaspoon of sea salt. Next, bring the mixture to a gentle boil over medium heat. After lowering heat to a simmer, cook, and stir sometimes until the chickpeas are tender;

after that drain and transfer to a large bowl. Now you should combine together garlic and salt to form a paste; place everything in a separate bowl and stir in vinegar, peppercorns, extra virgin olive oil and oregano. After pouring the garlic dress over the chickpeas and let stand for at least 35 minutes, just stirring one time. At the end, toss in scallions, bell pepper, cucumber, carrots, tomatoes, basil, and parsley. Serve warm.

Mediterranean Orzo Bowl

Total time: 25 minutes

Prep time: 5 minutes

Cook time: 20 minutes

Yield: 4 servings

Ingredients:

1 large egg

3minced garlic cloves

1 tablespoon extra-virgin olive oil

1 tablespoon of lemon juice1 pound ground turkey thigh

1/2 cup panko breadcrumbs

1 lemon zest

1 tablespoon chopped fresh dill (for meatballs)

1 teaspoon dried oregano

1/2 teaspoon ground cumin

1/4 teaspoon salt to season and to taste

1/4 teaspoon black pepper

2 tablespoons extra-virgin olive oil (for meatballs)

12 ounces orzo pasta

1 cut English cucumber

2 tablespoons fresh dill (just leaves)

1 pint halved grape tomatoes

1 1/2halved cups of pitted kalamata olives

1 thinly sliced red onion

12 ounces of store-bought tzatziki sauce

Directions:

First, make the meatballs in a medium bowl, where you will gently combine together the ground turkey, garlic, lemon zest, panko, egg, dill and season with, cumin, salt, oregano as well as pepper. With your hand create a mixture into 12 equal meatballs, each a mounded 2 tablespoons and start heating a large pot of water. After heating the olive oil for meatballs in a large skillet over medium-high heat. Go ahead and cook the meatballs through, until they are browned on both sides (10 minutes or more). Set aside and keep warm. In the meanwhile, cook the orzo in boiling water following to package directions until al dente. Drain, transfer to a bowl, and stir in the olive oil for orzo. Combine the lemon juice and dill for orzo to the remaining orzo, and toss to coat. At the end, season to taste with salt and pepper and serve with a side of tzatziki sauce.

Healthy Herbed Lamb

Total time: 40 minutes

Prep time: 5 minutes

Cook time: 35 minutes

Yield: 4 servings

Ingredients:

1 teaspoon of extra-virgin olive oil

1 chopped onion

½ cup of chopped pf rinsed, patted dry

8 ounces ground lamb

A pinch of salt and pepper

3 minced of garlic cloves

2 teaspoons of minced fresh marjoram

1 bay leaf 1 tablespoon chopped fresh dill

Lemon wedges

½ teaspoon dried

1 cup of rinsed medium-grind bulgur

1⅓ cups vegetable broth

Directions:

Heat oil in a large saucepan over medium-high heat until just smoking. Combine together salt, lamb and pepper and then cook, breaking up meat with a wooden spoon, until browned for a few minutes. Stir in onion and red peppers and cook until onion is softened, 5 to 7 minutes. Add garlic and marjoram and keep cooking until fragrant. After that stir in bulgur, broth, and bay leaf until simmer. Once reduced heat to low, cover, and simmer gently until bulgur is tender, it will probably take 20 minutes. Turn off the heat, lay a clean dish towel underneath the lid and let the bulgur sit for 10 minutes. Combine up dill and fluff gently with a fork to mix up. After seasoning with salt and pepper to taste, serve with lemon wedges.

Lemony Pork with Lentils

Total time: 45 minutes

Prep time: 15 minutes

Cook time: 30 minutes

Yield: 4 servings

Ingredients:

2 tablespoons of extra virgin olive oil

4 ounce of pork chops

2 tablespoons of fresh lemon juice

1 tablespoon of lemon zest

1 clove garlic

2 tablespoons of fresh rosemary

1 tablespoon of parsley

1 tablespoon of pure maple syrup

Water

½ cup green lentils

1 shallot 1 rib celery

½ cup of divided dry sherry

1 tablespoon of sea salt

1 tablespoon of unsalted butter

¼ tablespoon of red pepper flakes

Directions:

Firstly take a zipper bag and add extra virgin olive oil, lemon juice, lemon zest, garlic clove, pork chops,parsley,rosemary, and maple syrup, then refrigerate it for 10 hours. In the meanwhile combine together green lentils in a saucepan and water and set over medium heat. Cook lentils for at least 20 minutes until tender; drain and rinse. Before or after, preheat your oven to 350ºF and heat a nonstick skillet and add the marinade over medium high heat. Sear pork for a few minutes per side and transfer the skillet to the oven. While waiting, heat extra virgin olive oil to a second nonstick skillet over medium high heat; combine together shallot, red pepper flakes and celery and lower heat to medium and cook until tender. Stir in lentils until warmed through. After adding sea salt and sherry, cook for about 2 minutes until liquid is reduced by half. Next, stir in butter until melted. After that, divide the lentil mixture among four plates and top each serving with one pork chop from the first skillet. Discard garlic from marinade in the first skillet and deglaze the pan with cup sherry; increase heat and don't forget to add sea salt; again cook and stop only when the liquid is reduced by half. Evenly pour the sauce over each serving and serve hot.

Chorizo Pilau

Total time: 50 minutes

Prep time: 10 minutes

Cook time: 40 minutes

Yield: 4 servings

Ingredients:

1 tablespoon of extra virgin olive oil

1 large red onion, thinly sliced

1 tablespoon of smoked paprika

1 can of chopped tomatoes

¼ kg sliced of baby cooking chorizo

4 minced garlic cloves

¼ kg basmati rice

4 minced garlic cloves

½ chopped of liter stock

1 small bunch parsley

Zest of 1 lemon, peeled with its remainder wedged

2 fresh bay leaves

Directions:

Firstly place a thick saucepan on medium heat and pour in the oil and combine the onion and cook until you get the golden brown (it should be after 6 minutes or more). At this point, pour in the chorizo on the top of the onions to one side of the pan until it starts releasing some of its oils and then add the garlic and paprika. Cook it for 2 minutes, before adding the tomatoes and continue cooking for another 5 minutes. Pour in the rice, lemon zest, bay leaves and stock. Cook everything in the pan and bring to a boil. Combine the pan and simmer for 13 minutes. Turn down the heat, and cover the pan with foil, then put the lid back on and let it sit for about 15 minutes. Stir in the parsley and serve with lemon wedges. Squeezing the lemons makes the dish more amazing.

Tomato and Spinach Pasta

Total time: 35 minutes

Prep time: 10 minutes

Cook time: 25 minutes

Ingredients:

100g whole-wheat pasta

7.5ml extra virgin olive oil

½ sliced onion

60g drained can tomatoes,

60g frozen spinach

⅓ cup crumbled feta cheese

1g salt

1g ground pepper

Directions:

Follow package instructions to cook pasta in a pot of boiling water until al dente. In the meantime, add oil to a skillet set over medium heat; stir in onion and sauté for 3 minutes. Stir in tomatoes and simmer for about 10 minutes. Add spinach and cook until heated through. Drain the cooked pasta and toss with the sauce until well coated. Season with salt and pepper and serve topped with feta.

Mediterranean Soup

Chinese Noodle Soup

Total time: 20 minutes

Prep time: 5 minutes

Cook time: 15 minutes

Yield: 4 servings

Ingredients:

1 peeled onion

2 zucchini (medium size would be perfect)

2 tablespoons oil

4 ounces of thinly sliced shiitake mushrooms

1 teaspoon of minced fresh garlic

2 teaspoons of fresh ginger (peeled and finely grated)

1/2 teaspoon of Chinese 5 spice powder

Low sodium chicken broth

Total time: 45 minutes

Prep time: 10 minutes

Cook time: 35 minutes

Yield: 4 servings

Ingredients:

1/4 cup soy sauce

2 beaten eggs

2 tablespoons of chopped cilantro

1 tablespoon of lime juice

1/2 teaspoon of salt

Lime wedges

Chile sauce

Mung bean sprouts

Directions:

Start trimming the ends off onion and zucchini. Spiralize the other ingredients:½ cup onion, 6 cups zucchini. You can also use kitchen shears or a knife to cut the spirals into desired lengths. Then heat oil in a pot over medium heat. Mix mushroom, onion and cook, and stir for not more than 5 minutes. After it becomes soft and brown combine garlic, ginger and spice powder in it; keep stirring for 30 seconds. At this point, broth and soy sauce. Reduce heat to maintain a low simmer for more or less 20 minutes. When almost ready to serve, drizzle the beaten eggs into the soup in a thin stream with the cilantro as well as lime juice. Now it's time to cook the noodles: Heat a large skillet over medium heat and add 1 tablespoon of oil and a sprinkle of salt. Cook the noodles just for 3 minutes until they become soft. If necessary stir in order to release some juices. Divide and serve the noodles among 4 bowls before adding the soup. Enjoy your Asian-like soup.

Yummy Barley Soup

Total time: 1 hour 45 minutes

Prep time: 15 minutes

Cook time: 1 hour 30 minutes

Yield: 4 servings

Ingredients:

2 quarts vegetable broth

2 chopped stalks celery

2 large chopped carrots

1 cup barley

15 ounce can garbanzo beans, drained

1 chopped zucchini

14.5 ounce of can tomatoes with juice

1 chopped onion

1 tablespoon of paprika

1 tablespoon of curry powder

1 tablespoon of dried parsley

1 tablespoon of white sugar

3 bay leaves

1 tablespoon of garlic powder

1 tablespoon of Worcestershire sauce

½ tablespoon of ground black pepper

1 tablespoon of sea salt

Directions:

After adding broth to a large soup pot over medium heat, mix together all the ingredients mentioned above: celery, carrots, barley, garbanzo beans, zucchini, tomatoes, onion, bay leaves, parsley, sugar, garlic, powder, Worcestershire sauce, paprika, curry powder, sea salt and pepper. Place then this mixture to a gentle boil; cover and lower heat to medium low to cook for about 95 minutes until the soup becomes thick. Discard bay leaves and eat until it's hot.

Shellfish Soup

Total time: 50 minutes

Prep time: 15 minutes

Cook time: 35 minutes

Yield: 12 servings

Ingredients:

1 or 2 tablespoons of extra-virgin olive oil, plus extra for serving

12 ounces of peeled and deveined large shrimp

Shells reserved for 1 cup dry white wine or dry vermouth

Water as much as necessary

1½ pounds leeks only green parts sliced thin, and washed thoroughly

4 ounces of chopped pancetta

3 tablespoons tomato paste

2 garlic minced cloves

Salt and pepper

1 teaspoon grated fresh ginger

1 teaspoon ground coriander

½ teaspoon ground turmeric

⅛ teaspoon red pepper flakes

8-ounce of bottled clam juice

12 ounce large of sea scallops without tendons

12 ounces squid crosswise into ½- inch-thick rings

⅓ cup of minced fresh parsley

Directions:

Heat 1 tablespoon oil in the oven over medium heat until shimmering. After that mix together shrimp shells and cook, stirring often, until everything turns spotty brown and the pot starts to brown, (around 5 minutes). Add up wine and simmer; stirring something for a few minutes. After stirring in water, bring to simmer, and cook for another 5 minutes. Next, take a bowl and strain mixture through a fine-mesh strainer, in order to extract as much liquid as possible. Go ahead heating the remaining 1 tablespoon of oil in another pot over medium heat until shimmering. At this point, leeks and pancetta and cook until leeks are softened and lightly browned. It will probably take you 10 minutes. Stir again in tomato paste, combine garlic, 1 teaspoon salt, with ginger, coriander, turmeric, and pepper flakes and cook until fragrant. Now, stir in wine mixture and clam juice, scraping up any browned bits. For another 20 minutes simmer and cook until flavors meld. Then reduce heat to gentle simmer, add sea scallops, and cook for at least 3 minutes in total. It's also important to stir in shrimp and cook until just opaque throughout. Stir in squid, off the heat and cover with a kitchen towel, and let sit until just opaque and tender, for a few minutes. Finally, stir again, this time in parsley and season with salt and pepper to taste. Before serving, drizzle each portion with extra virgin oil.

Spicy Lentil Soup

Total time: 35 minutes

Prep time: 5 minutes

Cook time: 30 minutes

Yield: 4 to 6 servings

Ingredients:

2 tablespoons of extra virgin olive oil

1½ tablespoons of crushed red peppers

5 or 6 cups of water

1½ tablespoons of sumac

1½ tablespoons of cumin

1½ tablespoons of coriander Sea salt

1 large chopped yellow onion

1 large chopped garlic clove

2 tablespoons of dried mint flakes

Black pepper Pinch of sugar

1 tablespoons of flour

2 tablespoons of lime juice

1½ cups small brown lentils, rinsed

10-12 oz. frozen cut leaf spinach

2 cups chopped parsley

Directions:

Heat 2 tablespoons of extra virgin olive oil in a large ceramic pot over medium heat. After stirring in chopped onions and sauté for about 6 minutes until when it turns golden brown, you should combine garlic, dried mint, all spices, sugar and flour and cook for another few minutes making sure of stirring frequently. Go ahead stirring in water and broth in order to bring a rolling mixture over medium high heat; then stir in lentils and spinach and cook for about 6 minutes. At this point, lower heat to medium low for cooking and then covered,until lentils are tender (about 20 minutes). Finally, stir in chopped parsley and lime juice and turn off the heat. For the flavors, cover it for at least 5 minutes in order to meld it. You may serve with your favorite rustic Italian bread or in alternative a good idea could be pita bread.

Taco Soup

Total time: 50 minutes

Prep time: 15 minutes

Cook time: 35 minutes

Yield: 12 servings

Ingredients:

1.20 ounces taco seasoning

1 ounce ranch dip mix

1 1/2 pounds ground pork

2 diced onions

10 ounces diced tomatoes and green chiles

14.5 ounces stewed tomatoes

2 fresh tomatoes

14.5 ounces stewed tomatoes

16 ounces Ranch Style Beans

22 ounces of sweet corn

salt and pepper as much as necessary

tortilla chips

Diced avocado

Sour cream (as much as you desire)

Shredded cheddar cheese

Directions:

Take a large saucepan or small stockpot and heat over medium heat. After that, be ready to cook the pork, breaking it up with a spoon or spatula for about 10 minutes. Mix it with the onions, taco seasoning; keep stirring the tomatoes as well as the beans and corn. In case you need, add a small quantity of water to get your desired consistency. Proceed bringing a boil over medium-high heat, and then reduce to a simmer and cook for 15 minutes. It's highly preferable to cover it during the process of cooking. At the end, season with salt and pepper. Before serving the soup garnish it with chips, avocado, sour cream and cheese.

Soup with Tomato Pesto

Total time: 50 minutes

Prep time: 20 minutes

Cook time: 30 minutes

Yield: 6 servings

Ingredients:

Tomato Pesto Sauce 4-6 garlic cloves

1 cup diced tomatoes

15 large basil leaves

½ cup extra virgin olive oil

½ cup grated

Parmesan cheese

Sea salt Black pepper

Soup ingredients:

2 cups cooked white kidney beans

1 peeled and diced russet potato

1½ cups diced tomatoes

8-oz French green beans, chopped

6 cups vegetable broth

2 cups cooked red kidney beans

1 tablespoon of hot paprika 1 tbsp. coriander

2 tablespoons of extra virgin olive oil, plus more to taste

⅓ cup toasted pine nuts

Basil leaves Grated Parmesan

1 tablespoon of white vinegar

Sea salt Black pepper

Directions:

Firstly, start preparing tomato pesto sauce. Pulse together garlic and tomatoes in a food processor until combined properly. Apply basil and extra virgin oil and keep pulsing until smooth. After that, transfer the pesto to a bowl and stir in grated Parmesan cheese and add salt and pepper to taste. Set aside for the moment. In the meanwhile take a heavy pot or oven, and heat extra virgin olive oil over medium high heat. After adding diced potato, lower heat to medium to cook, and stir occasionally, for a few minutes. Combine together green beans, tomatoes, spices and vinegar and cover it. Continue cooking for another few minutes and then remove the lid. At this point raise heat to medium high; mix up vegetable broth and cook for about 5 minutes or more. After that lower heat again to medium and cover the pot. After cooking for about 12 minutes, stir in red and white kidney beans and keep cooking until the beans are heated through. Apply tomato pesto and remove the pot from heat. Place the soup into bowls and drizzle each extra virgin olive oil to taste, as well as grated Parmesan cheese, toasted pine nuts, and fresh basil leaves. Serve with Italian whole wheat bread.

Fresh Fish Soup

Total time: 50 minutes

Prep time: 15 minutes

Cook time: 35 minutes

Yield: 12 servings

Ingredients:

1 fennel bulb

1 tablespoon extra-virgin olive oil plus extra quantity for serving

6 ounces of chopped pancetta

2 celery ribs, halved and accurately cut into very small pieces

2 tablespoons of fronds minced discarded and cut into small pieces

1 chopped onion

4 minced of garlic cloves

1 teaspoon of paprika

1/8 teaspoon of red pepper flakes

8 ounces of bottled clam juice

Crumbled pinch saffron threads

1 cup dry white wine or dry vermouth

Salt and pepper as necessary

1 tablespoon of grated orange zest

Water

2 bay leaves

2 pounds skinless hake fillets

1½ sliced inches thick into 6 equal pieces

2 tablespoons of minced fresh parsley

Directions:

Heat oil in the oven over medium heat until shimmering, later add pancetta and cook, making sure of stirring occasionally. When it begins to brown, after 4 minutes, add up fennel pieces,1½ teaspoons salt as well as onion, celery, and cook until you see that vegetables are softened and lightly browned, for about 15 minutes. After stirring in garlic, paprika, pepper flakes, it's time to saffron and cook until fragrant, for a few seconds. At this point, add wine, scrap up any browned bits and mix with water, clam juice, and bay leaves.It's now necessary to bring to simmer and keep cooking until flavors meld, at least for 20 minutes. Turn off the heat and discard bay leaves. Nestle hack into cooking liquid; after covering, you should let sit until fish flakes apart when gently prodded with a paring knife and registers 140 degrees, for further 10 minutes. Finally, stir in orange zest, parsley, and fennel fronds break fish into large pieces. Before serving, season with salt and pepper to taste and drizzle individual portions with extra olive oil.

Meditteranean Meatball Soup with Saffron

Total time: 1 hour and 15 minutes

Prep time: 20 minutes

Cook time: 55 minutes

Yield: 6 to 8 servings

Ingredients:

2 slices hearty white sandwich bread cut in quarters

1 minced shallot

⅓ cup whole milk

8 ounces of ground pork

1 ounce of grated Manchego cheese

8 ounces of lean ground beef

3 tablespoons of minced fresh parsley

2 tablespoons of extra-virgin olive oil

½ teaspoon salt

½ teaspoon pepper

Ingredients for Soup:

1 teaspoon paprika

¼ crumbled teaspoon saffron threads

⅛ teaspoon red pepper flakes

1 tablespoon extra-virgin olive oil

1 chopped onion

1 red bell pepper, stemmed, seeded, and cut into small pieces

2 minced garlic cloves

Salt and pepper (necessary quantity)

1 cup of dry white wine

8 cups chicken broth

1 recipe Picada

2 tablespoons minced fresh parsley

Directions:

Use a fork and mash bread and milk together into a large bowl. Combine it with ground pork, Manchego, parsley, shallot, oil, salt, and pepper until it will blend. At this point, add ground beef and with your hands knead to make it combined. Pinch off and roll 2-teaspoon-size pieces of mixture into balls and place in a rimmed baking sheet (you may have 30 to 35 meatballs). Once you made them, cover with plastic wrap and refrigerate for at least 30 minutes. Now prepare the sopp. First of all, heat oil in a large oven over medium-high heat until it shimmers. Combine onion with bell pepper and cook until it turns soft and lightly browned, almost 10 minutes. After stirring in garlic, paprika, saffron, and pepper flakes and cook until for a few seconds it turns fragrant. Mix up in wine, scraping up any browned bits, and keep cooking for 1 or 2 minutes until almost completely evaporated. After stirring in broth, bring to simmer and add meatballs and simmer again it's completely cooked (almost 13 minutes). Off heat, mix in picada and parsley and season with salt and pepper to taste before serving it hot.

Tasty Lentil Soup

Total time: 1 hour 20 minutes

Prep time: 20 minutes

Cook time: 1 hour

Yield: 4 servings

Ingredients:

1 ½ cups brown lentils

¼ cup olive oil

¼ tablespoon of dried oregano

1 large chopped onion

2 dried bay leaves

1 tablespoon of tomato paste

2 pressed cloves garlic

1 chopped carrot

¼ tablespoon of dried rosemary

1 tablespoon of red wine vinegar

Directions:

Place the lentils in a large saucepan with water. Heat it over medium heat and bring to a boil; keep cooking for 20 minutes and don't forget to drain in a strainer. After that clean the saucepan and put olive oil and bring to medium heat. Combine the onions with the garlic and cook until the onions become soft enough, then add up the carrots and cook for a further 5 minutes. Cover the lentils with water, oregano, rosemary and bay leaves. When the pan comes to a boil, you need to reduce the heat and simmer for 10 minutes. Mix the tomato paste and keep simmering until the lentils soften. It would take half an hour. Finally, add water and regulate the consistency of soup you like the most. You may dizzle with the vinegar to taste.

Tasty Mediterranean Poultry Recipes

Coconut Chicken

Total time: 30 minutes

Prep time: 20 minutes

Cook time: 10 minutes

Yield: 4 servings

Ingredients:

20g shredded of coconut

1 small egg

100g chicken breast skinless

30g of almond flour

1 tablespoon of sea salt

7.5 ml coconut oil

Directions:

Combine shredded coconut, almond flour and sea salt in a bow. In a separate bowl, beat the egg; dip the chicken in the egg and roll in the flour mixture until it is properly coated. Combine coconut oil to a pan set over medium heat and fry the chicken until the crust begins to brown. After transfering the chicken to the oven, bake it at 350°F for about 10 minutes.

Roasted Chicken Pistachio and Currant Sauce

Total time: 50 minutes

Prep time: 15minutes

Cook time: 45 minutes

Yield: 4 servings

Ingredients:

3 sliced of shallots

Salt and pepper

½ cup fresh parsley leaves

6 tablespoons of water

5 tablespoons of extra-virgin olive oil

7 ounce of bone-in chicken thighs

1 tablespoon of lime juice

¼ cup dried currants

¼ cup of toasted shelled pistachios

¼ teaspoon orange blossom

½ teaspoon ground cinnamon

Directions:

First at all transfer rimmed baking sheet on lower rack, and heat oven to 450 degrees. At this point, toss shallots with 1 tablespoon of oil in a bowl. Cover and microwave for at least 5 minutes until when shallots are softened; from now on, stir once halfway through microwaving. Place shallots in the center of a 12-inch square of aluminum foil. Cover with a second square of foil and fold edges together to create a packet about 7 inches square; once done set aside. At this point, sti a metal skewer, poke the skin side of chicken thighs. Pat thighs dry with paper towels, rub skin with 1 tablespoon of oil, and season with salt and pepper. Place thighs skin side down on a hot sheet and place foil packet on upper rack. Roast chicken until you see that the skin side is brown and the chicken is around 160 degrees, for another 20 minutes, rotating sheet and removing foil packet after 10 minutes. Remove chicken from the oven and heat the broiler.

Flip chicken skin side up and broil on upper rack until skin is crisp and for 5 minutes well browned and chicken registers 175 degrees, rotating sheet as needed for even browning. Transfer chicken to a serving platter and let rest while preparing sauce. Pulsing shallots, parsley, water, currants, pistachios, lime juice, cinnamon, orange blossom water, and the teaspoon of salt in a food processor in order to make the finely chopped, about 10 pulses. While the processor is running, slowly drizzle in remaining 3 tablespoons of oil and process until incorporated. Scrape down sides of the bowl if needs be. Season with salt and pepper to taste. Serve chicken with sauce until it is hot.

Pan-Seared Chicken Breasts

Total time: 35 minutes

Prep time: 20 minutes

Cook time: 15 minutes

Yield: 4 servings

Ingredients:

6 tablespoons extra-virgin olive oil

¼ cup lemon juice or 2 lemons

½ teaspoon ground cumin

Salt and pepper

1 teaspoon honey

1 teaspoon smoked paprika

15 ounce of rinsed cans chickpeas

¼ cup chopped fresh mint

½ cup all-purpose flour

½ red onion, sliced thin

6 ounce of boneless chicken breasts

Directions:

Combine ¼ cup oil of lemon juice, honey, paprika, cumin, and ½ teaspoon salt, and ½ teaspoon pepper together in a large bowl. After that add chickpeas, onion, and mint to remaining dressing and toss to combine. Another important thing is to season with salt and pepper to taste and set aside for serving.Proceeding spread flour in a shallow dish. Beat thicker ends of chicken breasts rolled up in 2 sheets of plastic wrap. After patting chicken dry with paper towels don't forget to season with salt and pepper. Working with 1 chicken breast at a time, dredge in flour to coat, shaking off any excess. The final step consists of heating the remaining 2 tablespoons of oil in an inch skillet over medium-high heat and placing chicken in skillet and cooking, turning as well until it turns golden brown on both sides. Finally, transfer chicken to a serving platter, tent loosely with aluminum foil, and let rest from 5 to 10 minutes. Drizzle reserved dressing over chicken before serving with salad.

Chicken and Penne

Total time: 50 minutes

Prep time: 20 minutes

Cook time: 30 minutes

Yield: 4 servings

Ingredients:

1 package penne pasta

1 ½ tablespoon of butter

2 tablespoons of lemon juice

1 chopped tomato

3 tablespoons of chopped fresh parsley

½ cup of chopped red onion

1 tablespoon of dried oregano

¾ kg deboned and skinned chicken

1 can of artichoke soaked in water and chopped

2 pressed cloves garlic

½ cup feta cheese, crumbled

Sea salt Freshly ground black pepper

Directions:

Start cooking the penne pasta until al dente in a large saucepan with salted boiling water following the directions. Melt butter in a large skillet over medium heat and add the onions and garlic. Cook everything for 3 minutes and then combine the chicken to cook for about 6 minutes and stir often until the chicken is golden brown. After that, drain the artichoke hearts and add them to the skillet together with the cheese, lemon juice, tomatoes, oregano, parsley and drained pasta. It's now time to reduce the heat to medium low and keep cooking for additional 2 or 3 minutes. Combine the salt and pepper to taste and serve when it's still warm. Enjoy it!

Chicken with Roasted Vegetables

Total time: 55 minutes

Prep time: 15 minutes

Cook time: 40 minutes

Yield: 2 servings

Ingredients:

1 large zucchini, diagonally sliced

250g of sliced of baby new potatoes

6 firm halved plum tomatoes

1 rounded tablespoon of green pesto

3 tablespoons of extra virgin olive oil

1 red onion cut

1 seeded yellow pepper

12 black pitted olives

2 chicken breast fillets, skinless, boneless

Directions:

Preheat your oven to 400ºF. Mix zucchini, potatoes, tomatoes, onion, and pepper in a roasting pan and scatter with olives. Season with sea salt and black pepper. Place each chicken breast into four pieces and set them on top of the vegetables. Take a small bowl, mix pesto and extra virgin olive oil and spread over the chicken. Before preheating the oven for about 40 minutes, cover with foil and cook it. Uncover the pan and return to the oven; cook again for another 15 minutes and serve hot.

Braised Chicken with Mushrooms and Tomatoes

Total time: 60 minutes

Prep time: 15 minutes

Cook time: 45 minutes

Yield: 6 servings or more

Ingredients:

8 bone-in chicken thighs, trimmed Salt and pepper

1 tablespoon of extra-virgin olive oil

1½ tablespoons of all-purpose flour

1½ cups dry red wine

1 chopped onion

6 ounces of portobello mushroom caps cut into small pieces

4 garlic cloves, minced

2 teaspoons of minced fresh thyme

½ cup chicken broth

15 ounce of drained diced tomatoes

2 teaspoons of minced fresh sage

Parmesan cheese rind (optional)

Directions:

Preheat your oven at 300 degrees and pat chicken dry with paper towels and then season with salt and pepper. Heat oil in the oven over medium-high heat until smoking. Brown thighs off for 7 minutes per side. After transferring thighs to the plate, discard skin and drain 1 tablespoon of fat from the pot. Mix together onion, mushrooms, and salt to the fat left in the pot and cook, making sure of stirring sometimes until softened and beginning to brown, 9 minutes. After that, stir in garlic thyme and cook until fragrant,just for a few seconds. After stirring in flour and cook for a few minutes. After slowly whisk in wine, scraping up any browned bits and smoothing out any lumps. Stirring in broth, tomatoes, and cheese rind, if using, and bring to simmer. Place thighs into the pot, cover, and transfer to the oven. Cook until the chicken registers 195 degrees. It will take you 40 minutes more or less. At this point, remove the pot from the oven and transfer chicken to a serving platter. Before seasoning with salt and pepper, stir sage into sauce. Spoon sauce over chicken and serve.

Poultry Samosa

Total time: 50 minutes

Prep time: 15 minutes

Cook time: 35 minutes

Yield: 4 servings

Ingredients for wrappers:

2 tablespoons of unsalted butter

1 ½ cup all-purpose flour

A pinch of salt to taste

Water

For filling:

1 lb. mixed minced poultry (chicken, duck, turkey etc whatever you like)

¼ cup boiled peas

1 tablespoons of powdered ginger

1 or 2 green chilies that are finely chopped or mashed

½ tablespoons of cumin

1 tablespoons of coarsely crushed coriander

1 dry red chili broken into pieces

A small amount of salt (to taste)

½ tablespoon of dried mango powder

½ tablespoon of red chili powder

1-2 tablespoon of coriander.

Directions:

First start with the outer covering. Add the flour, butter and enough water to knead in a large bowl, and then into dough to make it stiff. Place everything into a container and leave it to rest for 5/10 minutes. In the meanwhile, place a pan on medium flame and add olive oil. At this point, roast the mustard seeds and once roasted, add the coriander seeds and the chopped dry red chilies. Combine all the dry ingredients for the filling and mix all the ingredients properly. Additionally, apply a little quantity of water and continue to stir the ingredients for another few minutes. Start making small balls out of the dough and roll them out. After cutting the rolled out dough into halves, add a little water on the edges to help you fold the halves into a cone. Add the filling to the cone and close up the samosa. While waiting, preheat your air fryer or the oven for around 6 minutes at 300 Fahrenheit. Cook at 200 degrees for another 20 to 25 minutes. For uniform cooking, open the basket and turn the samosas over around the halfway point. After this, fry at 250 degrees for another 10 minutes in order to give them the desired golden brown color and serve hot. For sides, I highly recommended you tamarind or mint chutney.

Chicken with Avocado Salad

Total time: 35 minutes

Prep time: 15 minutes

Cook time: 20 minutes

Yield: 4 servings

Ingredients:

500g breast fillets of chicken

2 tablespoons of extra virgin olive oil

1 small head of chopped broccoli

1 large peeled and diced avocado

2 slices of garlic cloves

1 large diced carrot

1/3 cup of currants

1 tablespoon of ground turmeric

3 tablespoon of ground cumin

1 1/2 cups chicken stock

1 1/2 cups couscous

A pinch of sea salt

Directions:

First at all, take a large frying pan where you can heat 1 tablespoon extra virgin olive oil over medium heat; then proceed adding chicken and cook through on both sides. At this point, transfer to a plate and keep warm. While waiting, mix together currants and couscous in a heatproof bowl; stir in boiling stock and set aside, in order to absorb the liquid you need to cover it for at least 6 minutes trying to separate the grains with a fork, for example. Next combine the remaining oil to a frying pan and add carrots;

cook, and continue stirring for a few minutes. Do the same and stir in broccoli, stir in garlic, turmeric, and cumin as well. After cooking for about 2 or 3 minutes remove the pan from heat. Finally, slice the chicken into small slices and mic the broccoli mixture; then toss to combine; season with a pinch of sea salt and serve with the avocado sprinkled on top of that.

Yummy Chicken Stew

Total time: 35 minutes

Prep time: 20 minutes

Cook time: 15 minutes

Yield: 4 servings

Ingredients:

1 tablespoon of extra virgin olive oil

3 chicken breast halves (8 ounces each), boneless, skinless, cut into small

pieces

A pinch of sea salt

Freshly ground pepper

1 medium onion, sliced

4 garlic cloves, sliced

½ tablespoon of dried oregano

1 ½ pounds escarole, ends trimmed, chopped

1 cup whole-wheat couscous, cooked

28 ounces of can whole peeled tomatoes, pureed

Directions:

Take a large heavy pot or even oven, and heat extra virgin olive oil over medium high heat. Proceed rubbing chicken with sea salt and pepper. At this point you may be ready to cook chicken in olive oil, tossing occasionally, for about 7 minutes or more. Remove the chicken from the heat when it turns brown and the transfer it to a plate and set aside. Mix together onion, garlic and oregano, tomatoes, sea salt and pepper to the pot and continue cooking for about 10 minutes until you see onions become lightly browned. In it combine the chicken and cook, covered for a few minutes in order that everything becomes opaque. At the end, fill the pot with escarole and cook again for about 4 or 5 minutes until tender. I recommend you to serve the chicken stew over couscous. Enjoy your meal.

Rosemary Chicken

Total time: 7 hours 20 minutes

Prep time: 20 minutes

Cook time: 7 hours, 10 minutes

Yield: 8 servings

Ingredients:

1 small onion thinly sliced

4 pressed cloves garlic

1 medium sliced red bell pepper

2 tablespoons of dried rosemary

½ tsp. dried oregano

2 pork sausages

8 skinned and deboned chicken breasts

¼ tablespoons of coarsely ground pepper

¼ cup dry vermouth

1 ½ tablespoons of cornstarch

2 tablespoons of cold water

Directions:

Start combining onion, garlic, bell pepper, rosemary and oregano in a slow cooker and then go ahead crumbling the sausages over the mixture, without forgetting to remove the casings. At this point, arrange the chicken in a single layer over the sausage and sprinkle it with pepper. It's now time to combine the vermouth and cook for 7 hours slow. Warm a deep platter, move the chicken to the platter and cover it. After adding the cornstarch with the water in a small bowl and adding this to the liquid in the slow cooker, increase the heat and cover. The process of cooking should be around 10 minutes.

Grilled Turkey with Salsa

Total time: 50 minutes

Prep time: 15 minutes

Cook time: 35 minutes

Yield: 6 servings

Ingredients for the spice rub:

1 ½ tablespoon of garlic powder

1 ½ tablespoon of sweet paprika

2 tablespoon of crushed fennel seeds

2 tablespoon of dark brown sugar

1 tablespoon of sea salt

1 ½ tablespoon of freshly ground black pepper

Ingredients for the salsa:

2 tablespoon of drained capers

¼ cup chopped pimento-stuffed green olives

2 diced scant cups cherry tomatoes

1 ½ tablespoon of extra virgin olive oil

1 large minced clove garlic

2 tablespoon of torn fresh basil leaves

2 tablespoon of fresh lemon juice

½ tablespoon of finely grated lemon zest

6 turkey breast cutlets

1 cup diced red onion

Sea salt Freshly ground black pepper as much as necessary

Directions:

First combine in a small bowl the garlic powder, with paprika, fennel seeds, brown sugar, salt and pepper. In another bowl, mix together the other ingredients: capers, olives, tomatoes, ¼ teaspoon sea salt and pepper as well as garlic, basil, onion extra virgin olive oil,lemon juice and zest and then set aside. After that, grill the meat on medium high heat after dipping in the spice rub for about 4 minutes per side until you see they are browned on both sides. Finally, transfer the grilled turkey to a serving plate and let rest for about 5 minutes. Serve with salsa.

Bisteeya

Total time: 25 minutes

Prep time: 10 minutes

Cook time: 15 minutes

Ingredients:

1 ½ cup almond flour

3 tablespoons of unsalted butter

2 tablespoons of powdered sugar

2 cups cold water

1 tablespoons of sliced cashew

Ingredients for filling:

2 cups minced chicken

1 cup sliced almonds

3 tablespoons of butter

Directions:

Combine together the ingredients in order to form a crumbly mixture. After that, knead the mixture with cold milk and wrap it gently. Roll the dough out into two large circles and press that dough into the pie tin and prick the sides with a fork. At this point, you should cook the ingredients for the filling on a low flame and pour into the tin. Cover the pie tin with the second round. Preheat your oven or the fryer to 300 Fahrenheit for a few minutes. During the process of cooking you should cover it. Once the pastry has turned golden brown, you will need to remove the tin and let it cool. At the end, cut into slices and serve with a dollop of cream.

Chicken and Eggs

Total time: 25 minutes

Prep time: 5 minutes

Cook time: 20 minutes

Ingredients:

Bread slices (white)

1 egg white for every 2 slices

1 tablespoon of sugar for every

2 slices of ½ lb. sliced chicken

Directions:

Put two slices and cut them along the diagonal. Take a bowl for whisking the egg whites with some sugar. After that, dip the bread triangles into this mixture and be ready to cook the chicken. Preheat your air fryer or your oven at 180° C for a few minutes. Start cooking at the same temperature for 20 minutes at least. For a uniform cook, halfway through the process, turn the triangles over so. Top with chicken and serve.

Gallette with Chicken

Total time: 55 minutes

Prep time: 15 minutes

Cook time: 40 minutes

Yield: 2 servings

Ingredients:

2 tablespoons of garam masala

A pinch of salt and pepper

1 lb. minced chicken

3 tablespoons of ginger chopped finely

1-2 tablespoons of fresh coriander leaves

2 or 3 green chopped chilies finely

1 ½ tablespoons of lemon juice

Directions:

Combine together all the ingredients in a clean bowl. Create flat galettes molding this mixture into round galettes. Make sure to wet them slightly with water. Preheat your air fryer or oven at 160 degrees Fahrenheit for at least 6 minutes. Place the galettes in the fry basket and let them cook for another 30 minutes at the same temperature. Continue rolling them over to get a uniform cook and then serve.

Honey Chili Chicken

Total time: 50 minutes

Prep time: 20 minutes

Cook time: 30 minutes

Yield: 4 servings

Ingredients for chicken fingers:

1 lb of chicken cut into slices

2 ½ tablespoons of ginger-garlic paste

1 tablespoons of red chili sauce

¼ tablespoon of salt

¼ tablespoon of red chili powder/black pepper

A few drops of edible orange food coloring

Ingredients for sauce:

2 tablespoons of olive oil 1 capsicum cut into long pieces

2 small onions cut into halves

1 ½ tablespoons of ginger garlic paste

½ tablespoons of red chili sauce

2 tablespoons of tomato ketchup

1 ½ tablespoons of sweet chili sauce

2 tablespoons of soya sauce

2 tablespoons of vinegar

1-2 tablespoons of honey

A pinch of black pepper

2 tablespoons of red chili flakes

Directions:

First at all, create the mix for the chicken fingers and theen coat the chicken well with it. Preheat your air fryer at 250 Fahrenheit for 7 minutes or your oven. After placing the fingers inside the basket, heat the temperature to 290 Fahrenheit for more or less another 20 minutes. Keep tossing the fingers occasionally during the cooking process so you will get a uniform cook. Mix up together all the ingredients mentioned above for making the sauce and cook it with the vegetables until it thickens. Finally, combine the chicken fingers to the sauce and cook everything until the flavors have blended. Serve and enjoy your food.

Mediterranean Meat Recipes

Prosciutto-Wrapped Dates

Total time: 15 minutes

Prep time: 10 minutes

Cook time: 5 minutes

Yield: 4 servings

Ingredients:

⅔ cup walnuts, toasted and chopped fine

½ cup minced fresh parsley

2 tablespoons of extra-virgin olive oil

½ teaspoon grated orange zest

Salt and pepper to taste

12 large pitted dates, halved lengthwise

12 thin slices prosciutto, halved lengthwise

Directions:

Take a bowl and combine together walnuts, oil, parsley and orange zest. After seasoning with salt and pepper. You should now mound one generous teaspoon of filling into the center of each date half. Wrapping prosciutto around dates carefully and you are ready to serve them. In case, you can let dates to room temperature before serving or refrigerate them for up to 8 hours.

Grilled pork

Total time: 45 minutes

Prep time: 5 minutes

Cook time: 40 minutes

Yield: 6 servings

Ingredients

2 lemons

5 peeled cloves garlic

4 pounds of boneless pork loin roast

1/4 cup of fresh sage leaves

1/3 cup of fresh rosemary leaves

1/4 cup of coarsely ground black pepper

1 tablespoon salt

Directions:

Pat pork roast dry and then take a bowl of food processor, where you will place remaining ingredients and process everything until fairly fine. After that, pat seasoning mixture over all surfaces of roast and turn on the heat on medium-hot grill. Close grill hood and grill for about more than 20 minutes per pound (the internal temperature on a thermometer should be around 145 degrees F). At this point, remove roast from heat and let rest about 11 minutes before slicing to serve with leftovers.

Yam Kebab

Total time: 30 minutes

Prep time: 5 minutes

Cook time: 25 minutes

Yield: 4 servings

Ingredients:

1 ½ tablespoons of ginger paste

1 ½ tablespoons of garlic paste

2 cups sliced yam

3 onions chopped

5 green chilies-roughly chopped

1 ½ tablespoons of salt

4 tablespoons of chopped coriander

3 tablespoons of cream

3 tablespoons of lemon juice

2 tablespoons of garam masala

2 ½ tablespoons of white sesame seeds

3 tablespoons of chopped capsicum

3 eggs

Directions:

First at all, grind all the ingredients mentioned above except for the egg and form a smooth paste with your hands. Next, coat the yam in the paste and then beat the eggs and apply a little salt to it. After dipping the coated vegetables in the egg mixture you already made you should transfer it to the sesame seeds and coat the yam. Transfer the vegetables on a stick and preheat your oven at 160 degrees Fahrenheit for a few minutes before cooking for another

25 minutes at the same temperature. Don't forget to turn the sticks over in between the cooking process to get a perfect cook on both sides.

Grilled flank steak with green sauce

Total time: 25 minutes

Prep time: 10 minutes

Cook time: 15 minutes

Yield: 4 servings

Ingredients:

1 pound eggplant sliced into thick planks

1 red onion, sliced into thick rounds

8 ounces cherry tomatoes

A pinch of salt and pepper

½ cup Italian Salsa Verde

2 sliced zucchini

2 tablespoons extra-virgin olive oil

1½ pounds flank steak, trimmed

Directions:

First at all, thread onion rounds from side to side onto two as well as cherry tomatoes onto two 12-inch metal skewers. Combine together onion rounds, zucchini, tomatoes, and eggplant with oil and season with salt and pepper. Open the bottom grill vent completely and light a large chimney starter filled with charcoal briquettes. Next, set and cook the grate in place, cover, and don't forget to open the lid vent. Heat grill until hot. If you use the gas grill you should turn all burners to high, cover, and heat the grill until it becomes hot. At this point, leave all burners on high. Transfer the steak with the onion, zucchini, tomato and eggplant on the grill to cook (covered if using gas), flipping steak and turning vegetables when it is necessary. Steak is well browned when it registers 120 to 125 degrees. At this point, transfer steak and vegetables to the carving board as they finish grilling and tent loosely with aluminum foil. Leave the steak at the room temperature for at least 10 minutes. While waiting, use tongs to slide tomatoes and onions off skewers. After cutting onion rounds, zucchini, and eggplant you should arrange vegetables on a serving platter and season with a pinch of salt and pepper. At the end, slice steak thin, arranging on a platter with vegetables and serve with sauce on top.

Italian Bean and Broth

Total time: 1 hour (soaking require 10 hours or more)

Prep time: 10 minutes

Cook time: 50 minutes

Yield: 8 servings

Ingredients:

Salt and pepper

8 ounces of dried cranberry beans, picked over and rinsed

1 tablespoon of extra virgin olive oil

2 ounces of chopped fine pancetta

1 leek of white and light green parts only, halved lengthwise, chopped fine, and washed thoroughly

1 chopped fine carrot

1 celery rib, chopped fine

1 zucchini, cut into small pieces

1 cup shredded red cabbage

1 small sprig fresh rosemary

Ingredients for Risotto:

2 tablespoons of extra-virgin olive oil

1 small chopped fine onion

2 thick slices of salami

6 ounces of meat

Salt and pepper

1½ cups of rice (carnaroli)

1 tablespoon of tomato paste

1 cup dry red wine

2 teaspoons of red wine vinegar

Directions:

Take a large container and dissolve 1½ tablespoons of salt. Go ahead and mix up beans and soak at room temperature for at least 10 hours or more. Don't forget to drain and rinse well. Next, heat oil over medium-high heat until it shimmers; combine pancetta and cook, stirring sometimes, until beginning to brown (5 minutes). Mix up leek, zucchini, and cabbage, carrot, celery, and keep cooking until they become soft and lightly browned (around 8 minutes). Sit in drained beans, rosemary, and a great quantity of water. After the water boils, reduce heat to medium-low, cover, and simmer, stirring occasionally. When finally the beans are tender, you should strain into a large bowl the previous mixture through a fine-mesh strainer. Discarding rosemary and transfer bean-vegetable mixture to another bowl; set aside. After that, cover, and keep warm over low heat. At this point, prepare risotto. In order to do that, heat 1 tablespoon of oil in the oven over medium heat until it shimmers. Mix up onion, salami, as well as salt and cook until onion is softened for a few minutes. After adding rice and cooking, stir frequently. You also need to stir in tomato paste and cook adding wine and keep stirring more frequently, until fully absorbed. Go ahead stir in 2 cups of warm broth, bring to a simmer, and cook, stirring occasionally, until almost fully absorbed, about 5 minutes.

Keep cooking rice, stirring frequently and adding warm broth, 1 cup at a time, every few minutes. Once the rice became creamy and cooked through but still firm in center, (around 15 minutes). Turn down the heat, stir in bean-vegetable mixture, cover, and let sit for another 5 minutes. Adjust consistency applying oil and vinegar and season with salt and pepper to taste. Serve and enjoy it.

Pork sticks

Total time: 25 minutes

Prep time: 5 minutes

Cook time: 20 minutes

Yield: 2 servings

Ingredients:

1 lb. boneless pork cut into fingers

2 cup of dry breadcrumbs

2 tablespoons of oregano

2 tablespoons of red chili flakes

Ingredients for marinade:

1 tablespoon of red chili powder

6 tablespoons of corn flour

4 eggs

1 ½ tablespoon of ginger-garlic paste

4 tablespoons of lemon juice

2 tablespoons of salt

1 tablespoon of pepper powder

Directions:

Combine all the ingredients for the marinade and put the pork fingers inside and let it rest overnight. After combining oregano with the breadcrumbs, and red chili flakes transfer the marinated fingers on this mixture. Use a plastic wrap to cover it and leave it like that until you have to start cooking it. At this point, preheat your oven (or your airfryer) at 160 degrees Fahrenheit from 5 or 10 minutes. Transfer the pork fingers in the oven and cook at the same temperature for another 15 minutes or so. Don't forget to toss occasionally the fingers so that they can be cooked uniformly. Once it's ready you can serve and enjoy your delicious meal.

Seasoned Lamb Burgers

Total time: 30 minutes

Prep time: 20 minutes

Cook time: 10 minutes

Yield: 4 servings

Ingredients:

1 ½ pounds ground lamb

1 tablespoon of ground cumin

1 8 oz of package plain Greek yogurt

¼ cup fresh cilantro

½ tablespoon of ground cinnamon

1 small clove garlic, pressed

¾ tablespoon of red pepper flakes, crushed

¼ cup fresh flat leaf parsley

1 tablespoon of ground ginger

¼ cup extra virgin olive oil, divided

1 tablespoon of black pepper, freshly ground; divided

Sliced tomato

1 tablespoon of sherry vinegar

2 tablespoon of fresh oregano

2 pitas, warmed and halved

Directions:

First at all prepare a charcoal or gas grill fire. Combine the ground lamb with cumin, ginger, cinnamon, 1 tablespoon of extra virgin olive oil as well as black pepper. Mix gently and divide this into four burgers. After spraying the grill with some extra olive oil, go ahead and grill the burgers for at least 5 minutes on each side. Add the rest of the olive oil, oregano, garlic, cilantro, red pepper flakes, parsley and vinegar in a food processor. Once it forms a thick paste you can put each burger in pita bread on a plate with sliced tomato, applying the processed sauce and a serving of yogurt. Enjoy it!

Green Curry Beef

Total time: 1 hour, 20 minutes

Prep time: 10 minutes

Resting time: 30 minutes

Cook time: 40 minutes

Yield: 3 servings

Ingredients:

2 sliced thinly cloves garlic

¼ tablespoon of turmeric

½ tablespoon of ground cumin

½ cup chopped parsley

1 cup cilantro leaves

1 chopped white onion,

1 fresh chopped Thai green chili

1 can light coconut milk

1/4 tsp. turmeric

1/2 tablespoons of ground cumin

¼ tablespoon of sea salt

1 tablespoon of extra virgin olive oil

2 tablespoons of lime juice

¼ tablespoon of sea salt

Black pepper

16 ounces of beef cut into small pieces

Directions:

For green curry paste, you should take a food processor, combine together cilantro, onion, extra virgin olive oil, lime juice, parsley, turmeric, cumin, chili pepper, garlic, sea salt, and pepper and process until very smooth. Add beef and green curry paste in a bowl and toss to coat. After refrigerating for at least 30 minutes. Once ready, heat a large skillet over medium high heat and mix beef as well as the green curry sauce. Lower heat and stir for about 10/12 minutes. When the meat becomes browned on the outside means it's time to stir in coconut milk and cook for about 30 minutes until you see the sauce is thick. Serve immediately and enjoy your meal!

Healthy Lamb

Ingredients:

1 onion cut it into quarters

5 tbsp. gram flour

2 cups sliced lamb

A pinch of salt to taste

1 big capsicum cut into big cubes

Ingredients for the filling:

2 cup fresh green coriander

½ cup mint leaves

2 tablespoons of ginger-garlic paste

4 tablespoons of fennel

3 tablespoons of lemon juice

1 small onion

7 flakes garlic

A pinch of salt to taste

Directions:

First prepare the chutney adding the ingredients to a blender and make a thick paste. After slitting the pieces of lamb, stuff half the paste into the cavity obtained. At this point you should have the paste's remaining that can be added to the gram flour and then salt. After tossing the pieces of lamb in this mixture it's time to set aside. Drizzle a little bit of the mixture over the capsicum and onion and transfer these to a stick along with the lamb pieces. Preheat your oven at 290 Fahrenheit for about 5-10 minutes and cook the sticks with the lamb at 180 degrees for around half an hour. On the other hand, the sticks with the vegetables need to be cooked at the same temperature for just 8 minutes. To provide a uniform cook, turn the sticks in between in order to let each side not get burnt. Serve and enjoy it.

Italian Carpaccio

Total time: 45 minutes

Prep time: 45 minutes

Cook time: 0 minutes

Yield: 2 servings

Ingredients:

2 teaspoons of mustard

Salt and pepper to taste

1 pound steak (tenderloin)

Sea salt and black pepper

1 ounce of Parmigiano-Reggiano

1 tablespoon balsamic vinegar

2 tablespoons olive oil

1 cup baby arugula leaves

Directions:

Take a small bowl and whisk together all the ingredients above. Then slice the steak as thin as possible and arrange the arugula on two plates, topping with beef slices. Season with sea salt and black pepper. Before serving, garnish with shavings of Parmigiano.

Healthy Mediterranean Desserts

Apricot Spoon

Total time: 2 hours, 10 minutes

Cook time: 10 minutes

Refrigerator time: 2 hours

Yield: 4 servings

Ingredients:

1½ cups sugar

1 cup honey

Water

1½ pounds ripe but firm apricots cut into small wedges

2 tablespoons lemon juice

Directions:

Combine sugar, honey, and water to boil in the oven over high heat. Keep cooking, and stirring sometimes. Syrup should measure 2 cups, about 15 minutes. Add apricots and lemon juice and then return to boil. After reducing the heat to medium-low and simmer, stir often until apricots soften and release their juice, (about 7 minutes). Turn off the heat and let it cool to room temperature completely. At the end, transfer apricots and syrup to an airtight container and refrigerate for 1 day before serving. Fruit may also be refrigerated for up to 1 week.

Strawberry Pudding

Total time: 25 minutes

Prep time: 5 minutes

Cook time: 20 minutes

Yield: 4 servings

Ingredients:

1 cup strawberry juice

2 cups milk

3 tablespoons of unsalted butter

1 cup strawberry slices

2 tablespoons of custard powder

3 tablespoons of powdered sugar

Directions:

Preheat your oven or airfryer to 300 Fahrenheit for 6 minutes. Then take a pan where you can boil the milk and the sugar. Add the custard powder as well as the strawberry juice and stir until the mixture becomes thick. After that, place the dish in the basket and reduce the temperature to 250 Fahrenheit. Cook for 12 minutes and set aside to cool. After garnishing with strawberry, serve and enjoy it.

Rhubarb Pancakes

Total time: 15 minutes

Prep time: 5 minutes

Cook time: 10 minutes

Yield: 2 servings

Ingredients:

1 cup shredded rhubarb

1 ½ cups almond flour

3 eggs

2 tablespoons of dried basil

2 tablespoons of dried parsley

Salt and Pepper to taste

3 tablespoons of Butter

Directions:

Preheat your air fryer or oven to 250 Fahrenheit. Take a small bowl, where you can combine together all the ingredients to get a smooth and well balanced mixture. After that, take a pancake mold and grease it with butter. Apply the batter to the mold and cook until both the sides of the pancake have browned on both sides and serve hot.

Citrus Tarts

Total time: 40 minutes

Prep time: 15 minutes

Cook time: 25 minutes

Yield: 6 servings

Ingredients

1 ½ packs frozen mini phyllo pastry shells

1 cup whipping cream, divided

½ tsp. almond extract, divided

¼ cup orange curd

¼ cup strawberry curd

Fresh mint leaves for garnish

Directions:

First bake the pastry shells following the package's instructions and set aside until completely cool. Take a food processor, where you can beat ½ cup whipping cream, almond extract and orange curd. When you get soft peaks you can spoon this mixture into half the baked pastry shells. Keep beating the remaining whipping cream in the food processor until soft peaks and then spoon in the remaining shells. Garnish with mint leaves and serve.

Berry Bliss

Total time: 5 minutes

Yields: 2 servings

Ingredients:

2 cups plain low-fat

1 cup frozen strawberries

1 frozen banana

Greek yogurt

1 cup frozen blueberries

1 tablespoon of flaxseed

2 tablespoon of almond butter

Directions:

Combine together all ingredients mentioned above in a blender and blend until smooth. Serve and enjoy it.

Delicious Sweet Cherries

Total time: 2 hours, 10 minutes

Cook time: 10 minutes

Refrigerator time: 2 hours

Yield: 4 servings

Ingredients:

½ kg of pitted fresh cherries

3 stripes of orange zest

3 strips lemon zest

Water as much as you need

¾ cup sugar

15 peppercorns

1 split small vanilla bean

Directions:

First, set the cherries aside, adding the rest of the ingredients to a saucepan and bring to a boil, stirring frequently until all the sugar is dissolved. At this point, combine together the cherries and simmer for about 10/12 minutes and stop before disintegrating. At this point, pour out the foam on the surface and set aside to cool. Let cool in the fridge for about 2 hours. Before serving, strain the liquid. A good idea is to enjoy it with ice cream.

Dried Fruit dessert

Total time: 2 hours, 10 minutes

Cook time: 10 minutes

Refrigerator time: 2 hours

Yield: 4 servings

Ingredients:

Water

2 sticks cinnamon

2 ounces of dried stemmed Turkish or Calimyrna figs

3 tablespoons honey

1 tablespoon juice

1¼ teaspoons ground coriander

2 inch of strips lemon zest

¾ cup dried apricot

½ cup dried cherries.

Directions:

Take a large saucepan and boil water in over medium-high heat and add cinnamon sticks, honey, lemon zest and juice, and coriander. Cook, and stir occasionally, until honey has dissolved, about 4 minutes. After that stir in figs and apricots and return to boil. Be careful to reduce heat to medium-low and simmer. Stir sometimes. When the fruit is plump and tender, after 30 minutes you should start stirring in cherries and cook until cherries are plump and tender. Figs should have broken apart, while liquid is thickened and syrupy. Once ready, turn down the heat and discard lemon zest and cinnamon sticks. Let the mixture cool slightly and then serve warm, at room temperature, or chilled if you want.

Cherry Pancakes

Total time: 10 minutes

Prep time: 5 minutes

Cooking time: 5 minutes

Ingredients:

2 tbsp. sliced cherries

1 ½ cups almond flour

3 eggs

2 tsp. dried basil

2 tsp. dried parsley

Salt and Pepper to taste

3 tbsp. Butter

Directions:

Start preheating your air fryer or oven to 250 Fahrenheit. Take a small bowl where you can combine together all the ingredients making sure that the mixture is smooth and balanced. Grease butter in a pancake mold and mix up the batter to the mold and place it in the oven to cook until both the sides of the pancake have browned properly. Then serve with maple syrup.

Nutty Banana Oatmeal

Total time: 15 minutes

Prep time: 10 minutes

Cook time: 5 minutes

Yield: 4 servings

Ingredients:

¼ cup quick cooking oats

3 tablespoons of raw honey

½ cup skim milk

2 tablespoons of chopped walnuts

1 tablespoons of flax seeds

1 peeled banana

Directions:

Take a microwave-safe bowl, where you can combine oats, milk, walnuts, honey, and flaxseeds; microwave on high for about 2 minutes. While waiting, take a small bowl, and try to mash the banana with a fork until you get a fine consistency; stir into the oatmeal and serve immediately.

Pumpkin Smoothie

Total time: 15 minutes

Yield: 2 servings

Ingredients:

⅓ cup of low-fat

Greek yogurt

½ tablespoons of cinnamon

2 tablespoons of vanilla extract

½ cup skim milk

½ cup ice, crushed

½ cup pumpkin butter

2 tablespoons of maple syrup

Directions:

Mix up all ingredients in a blender and blend until smooth. Serve in a tall glass with a straw.

Lemon biscuits

Total time: 15 minutes

Prep time: 10 minutes

Cook time: 5 minutes

Yield: 4 servings

Ingredients:

¼ teaspoon salt

1 tablespoon of anise seeds

¼ teaspoon vanilla extract

7 ounces of sugar

2 large eggs

1 tablespoon of grated lemon zest

10 ounces of all-purpose flour

1 teaspoon baking powder

Directions:

First adjust oven rack to middle position and heat oven to 350 degrees. Draw two 13 by 2-inch rectangles,spaced 3 inches apart, with a ruler and pencil, on a piece of parchment paper. Before placing the parchment on it, grease the baking sheet and marked side down. In a small bowl, whisk flour, baking powder, and salt together while in a more large bowl, you need to whisk sugar and eggs until pale yellow. Next, whisk in lemon zest, anise seeds, and vanilla until combined well. Using rubber spatula, stir in flour mixture, combine and divide dough in half. Using lines on parchment as guide and your floured hands, form each half into a small rectangle. Use rubber spatula lightly coated with vegetable oil spray, smooth tops and sides of loaves and keep baking until loaves are golden. After that crack on top, for about 35 minutes, rotate the sheet halfway through the process. Let loaves cool on a sheet to a room temperature for 15 minutes, then transfer to a cutting board. Reduce oven temperature to 325 degrees and with a serrated knife, slice each loaf on slight bias into thicker slices. At this point, arrange cookies cut side down on a sheet and bake until crisp and golden brown on both sides, (probably around 15 or 20 minute) making sure to flip cookies halfway through baking. Let cool completely on the wire rack and then be ready to serve. You can store these biscuits at room temperature for up to 1 month.

Banana Pudding

Total time: 15 minutes

Prep time: 5 minutes

Cook time:10 minutes

Yield: 4 servings

Ingredients:

1 cup banana juice

2 tablespoons of custard powder

3 tablespoons of powdered sugar

2 cups milk

3 tablespoons of chopped mixed nuts

3 tablespoons of unsalted butter

Directions:

Preheat your oven or airfryer to 300 Fahrenheit for a few minutes. After that, boil the milk and the sugar in a pan together with the custard powder followed by the banana juice and stir. When you get a thick mixture you can transfer everything in the oven and reduce the temperature to 250 Fahrenheit. Cook for about 10 minutes and set aside to cool. After garnishing with nuts, serve and enjoy it.

Pistachio and Fruits

Total time: 12 minutes

Prep time: 5 minutes

Cook time: 7 minutes

Yield: 12 servings

Ingredients:

1 ¼ roasted cups unsalted pistachios

2 tablespoons of sugar

¼ tablespoon of allspice

½ cup of chopped and dried apricots

¼ tablespoon of ground nutmeg

¼ cup dried cranberries

½ tablespoons of cinnamon

Directions:

Preheat your oven to 350°F. After that bake pistachios in a baking tray for about 7 minutes or more. Set aside and let them cool completely. Combine together all the ingredients mentioned above in a bowl. When the mix is well combined and you are ready to serve.

BONUS: Mix mediterranean healthy, easy and delicious recipes

Week 1

Lamb Barbecue Club Sandwich

Total time: 40 minutes

Prep time: 10 minutes

Cooking time: 30 minutes

Yield: 2 servings

Ingredients:

2 slices of white bread

1 tablespoon of softened butter

½ lb. of cut lamb cut into cubes

1 small capsicum

Ingredients for Barbeque Sauce:

¼ tablespoon of Worcestershire sauce

½ tsp. olive oil

½ flake garlic crushed

¼ cup chopped onion

½ tablespoon of sugar

¼ tablespoon of red chili sauce

Directions:

Firstly remove the edges from the slices of bread and then cut the slices horizontally. After that, cook the ingredients for the sauce until it thickens. At this point, add the lamb to the sauce and stir till it obtains the flavors. At the same time, roast the capsicum and peel the skin off. After cutting the capsicum into slices, mix all the ingredients together and apply it to the bread slices. Now or even a bit before preheat your Air Fryer for 5 minutes at 300 Fahrenheit or cook in the oven. Transfer everything in it and cook until it's ready. In both cases make sure of preparing the sandwiches in a way that no two sandwiches are touching each other. Continue at 250 degrees for around 15/20 minutes making sure to turn the sandwiches in between the cooking process to cook both slices. Serve the sandwiches with tomato ketchup or your favorite sauces.

Garlicky Scrambled Eggs

Total time: 25 minutes

Prep time: 10 minutes

Cooking time: 15 minutes

Yield: 2 servings

Ingredients:

½ tablespoons of extra virgin olive oil

½ cup ground beef

½ tsp. garlic powder

3 eggs Salt Pepper

Ingredients:

Arrange a medium-sized pan over medium heat. Put extra virgin olive oil and heat until hot but not smoking or you have to redo it again. After that, stir in ground beef and cook for about 10 minutes or until almost done. Stir in garlic and sauté for about 3 or 4 minutes. Thereafter, take a large bowl, beat the eggs until almost frothy; season with salt and pepper. Put the egg mixture to the pan with the cooked beef and scramble until ready. I recommend you to serve with toasted bread and olives, for a healthier breakfast or branch.

Pasta Fusilli with Almond–Arugula Pesto

Total time: 15 minutes

Prep time: 5 minutes

Cook time: 10 minutes

Yield: 7 or 8 servings

Ingredients:

1 pound of whole-wheat fusilli or any short quinoa pasta

3 cups fresh baby arugula

2 cloves garlic

¼ cup blanched almonds

¼ cup good-quality extra virgin olive oil (unfiltered, if possible)

¼ cup grated Parmigiano Reggiano cheese

¼ cup grated Pecorino Romano cheese

240 g of cherry tomatoes, halved

Directions:

Cook the pasta Fusilli according to package directions, until al dente around (10/11 minutes) and then drain, reserving ½ cup of pasta water. Mix the ingredients (arugula, garlic, and almonds) in a food processor and go ahead until chopped. Additionally, pour olive oil into the processor. At this point, add some pasta water if necessary to thin out. Spoon the pesto into a medium bowl. Don't forget to stir in the Parmigiano and Pecorino cheeses as well as the pesto into the pasta. Finally add everything in cherry tomatoes. Mix well to combine and serve hot.

Cream Sandwiches

Total time: 15 minutes

Prep time: 10 minutes

Cook time: 5 minutes

Yield: 4 servings

Ingredients:

2 tablespoons finely chopped black olives, oil-cured

¼ cup chopped fresh basil leaves

1 small zucchini, thinly sliced

½ cup mayonnaise and Olive Oil cut and divided

8 slices whole-wheat bread

4 slices of bacon

4 slices provolone cheese

7 oz. roasted red peppers, sliced

Directions:

Take a small bowl, combine olives, basil, and the cup of mayonnaise; evenly spread the mayonnaise mixture on the bread slices and layer slices with bacon, zucchini, provolone and peppers. Fill the remaining bread slices and spread the remaining mayonnaise on the outside of your sandwiches. At this point, cook over medium heat for 5 minutes or more, turning once, until the cheese is well melted and the sandwiches are golden brown.

Egg Veggie Scramble

Total time: 30 minutes

Prep time 15 minutes

Cook time 15 minutes

Yield: 2 servings

Ingredients:

2 tablespoons of extra virgin olive oil

1 medium orange bell pepper, diced

½ cup frozen corn kernels

1 scallion, thinly sliced

¼ tablespoon of cumin, freshly ground

¼ tsp. allspice, plus a pinch

2 egg whites

Pinch of cinnamon

⅓ cup white cheddar, shredded

1 medium avocado, diced

½ cup fresh salsa

2 whole-wheat flour tortillas, warmed

Directions:

Heat a teaspoon of olive oil in a nonstick pan over medium heat. Add bell pepper, mixing and turning for a few minutes until soft; then add up the corn, scallion, cumin, as well as the spice and cook for another few minutes until the scallion wilts. Transfer it to a plate and cover it with foil. Wipe the pan clean with a paper towel and set it aside. Place the eggs and their whites in a bowl; whisk them together energetically with the water, a pinch of allspice and a pinch of cinnamon. For the remaining olive oil, heat it in the pan over medium heat and put the egg mixture. Cook until the bottom sets, about 30 seconds, then stir gently. Keep stirring for about 3 minutes, then combine the shredded cheese and vegetables with what you had wrapped in foil before. Before serving add avocado, salsa and the tortillas.

Spanish Paella (Arroz en Paella)

This is a spanish seafood "party in a pot" which is said to be a descendant of a similar dish originating in the Arabian Peninsula.

Ingredients:

2 tablespoons (30 ml) extra-virgin olive oil

1 yellow onion, diced

2 tablespoons (32 g) tomato paste

¼ pound (115 g) jumbo shrimp, deveined and peeled 1 pound

450 g of a sliced baby squid

¼ pound of boneless white fish fillet cut into 2-inch pieces or smaller

2 cups of medium-grain Spanish rice

Pinch of good-quality saffron

2 or 3 teaspoons sweet paprika

1 clove garlic, minced

2 tablespoons (9 g)

1 teaspoon kosher salt

¼ cup of jarred pimiento peppers

Yield: 8 servings

Directions:

Heat the oil in a large wide skillet over medium heat. After that add the onion and cook until golden brown, about 5 minutes or more. Combine the tomato paste, and then stir slowly so that the paste would blend with onion and oil. Add all the fishes to the pan. Cook until barely opaque, 3 to 5 minutes. After adding the rice and stir in the saffron, paprika, garlic, and parsley it is the moment to pour the stock over the top of the mixture and add salt. In order to bring to a boil increase heat, and then reduce heat to low, and stir. Cook your paella, and then let it uncovered for 35 minutes or more until when you see all the liquid absorbed. Only occasionally stir. When the paella is done, allow it to stand at room temperature for 12 minutes. Serve warm after garnishing with pimientos.

Mediterranean Breakfast Wrap

Total time: 10 minutes

Prep time: 5 minutes

Cooking time: 5 minutes

Yield: 2 servings

Ingredients:

½ cup fresh-picked spinach

4 egg whites

A few sun-dried tomatoes

2/3 mixed-grain flax wraps

½ cup feta cheese crumbles

Directions:

Arrange anche cook spinach, egg whites and tomatoes in a frying pan for about 4 minutes or until lightly browned. Make sure to flip it over and cook the other side for 4 minutes or until almost done. You can microwave the wraps for about 15 seconds; after taking from the microwave, fill each wrap with the egg mixture, sprinkle with feta cheese crumbles and roll up. Cut each wrap into two parts and enjoy your meal.

Week 2

Herbed lamb cutlets with Mediterranean vegetables

Total time: 60 minutes

Prep time: 15 minutes

Cook time: 45 minutes

Yield: 4 servings

Ingredients:

2 peppers deseeded and cut into pieces

1 large sweet potato peeled and cut into pieces

2 courgettes sliced into chunks

1 red onion cut into wedges

1 tablespoon of extra virgin olive oil

8 lean lamb cutlets

1 tablespoon of chopped thyme leaf

2 tablespoon of chopped mint leaves

Directions:

Start preheating your oven to 220°. In the meanwhile, put the peppers, sweet potato, courgettes and onion on a large baking tray and drizzle over the oil. After seasoning with lots of ground black pepper, roast it for around 25 or 30 minutes. Next, trim the lamb of as much fat as possible mixing the herbs with a few twists of ground black pepper and pat all over the lamb. Remove the vegetables from the oven, turn them over and push to one side of your tray. Lately, you need to place the cutlets on the hot tray to return to the oven for another 10 minutes or more. Don't forget to turn the cutlets and cook for a further 10 minutes. Both the vegetables and lamb must be tender and lightly charred. Once cooked, put everything on the tray and serve warm.

Seasonal Fruit Platter

Total time: 10 minutes

Prep time: 10 minutes

Cook time: 0 minutes

Yield: 6 servings

Ingredients:

2 cups of fresh strawberries

1 cup of chopped fresh cantaloupe

1 cup of chopped fresh honeydew melon

1 cup of chopped fresh pineapple peeled and diced

8 kiwi, peeled and sliced

Directions:

Prepare and place all the fruit in a good pattern on a serving plate and serve with cocktail forks or cocktail toothpicks.

Moroccan Bread

Total time: 55/60 minutes

Prep time: 10 minutes

Cook time: 45minutes

Yield: 3 servings

Ingredients:

1 tablespoon of active, dry yeast

2 teaspoons sugar 1 teaspoon kosher salt

7 cups of wholewheat or barley flour, plus extra for kneading

4 teaspoons of extra-virgin olive oil, divided

3 teaspoons of sesame seeds

Yield: 3 serving

Directions:

Pour the warm water into the bowl of a standing electric mixer with a paddle attachment, and then sprinkle the yeast and sugar over the water, and mix until dissolved. Add the salt and gradually mix in 6 cups of flour, adding up one cup at a time for a maxim of 2 cups, until dough pulls away from the side of the bowl. Switch to a hook attachment and knead for about 5 minutes on medium speed until smooth. Roll the dough into a 12-inch log, then divide into three equal pieces. Create a 4-inch dome-shaped loaf with that. Place loaves on a baking sheet greased with olive oil. Place it in a draft-free area covered with a towel to rise for around 1 hour until doubled. While waiting, preheat the oven to 350°F and uncover the loaves and brush each with 1 teaspoon olive oil and 1 teaspoon sesame seeds. Bake for 20 to 30 minutes, until sufficiently lightly golden. Let cool slightly, and serve warm.

The alternative is gluten-free: for preparing that instead of using the whole-wheat flour try the cups of brown rice flour, 1 cup of tapioca flour, 2 cups sorghum flour, and 2 teaspoons xanthan gum.

Fresh Frittata

Total time: 30 minutes

Prep time: 10 minutes

Cook time: 15 minutes

Yield: 4 servings

Ingredients:

3 or 4 tablespoons of extra virgin olive oil, divided

1 cup chopped onion

2 cloves garlic, minced

8 or 9 eggs, beaten

¼ cup half-and-half, milk or light cream

½ cup sliced Kalamata olives

½ cup roasted red sweet peppers, chopped as well as ½ cup crumbled feta cheese

⅛ tablespoon of black pepper

¼ cup fresh basil

2 tablespoon of Parmesan cheese, finely shredded

½ cup coarsely crushed onion-and-garlic croutons

Fresh basil leaves, to garnish

Directions:

The first thing to do is preheat your broiler. Heat extra virgin olive oil in a broiler-proof skillet set over medium heat; sauté onion and garlic for a few minutes since it will become tender. While waiting, beat eggs and half-and-half in a bowl until well combined. Now stir in olives, roasted sweet pepper, feta cheese, black pepper and basil. At this point, pour the egg mixture over the sautéed onion mixture and cook until almost set. Lift the egg mixture to allow the uncooked part to flow underneath with a spatula. Continue cooking for a few minutes. Finish combining the remaining extra virgin olive oil, Parmesan cheese, and crushed croutons in a bowl; sprinkle the mixture over the frittata and broil for about 6 minutes or until the crumbs are golden and the top is set. To serve, cut the frittata into wedges and garnish with fresh basil.

Cheesy Potato Wedges

Total time: 25 minutes

Prep time: 5 minutes

Cook time: 20 minutes

Yield: 1 or 2 servings

Ingredients:

2 medium sized potatoes cut into wedges

Ingredients for the marinade:

1 tablespoons of olive oil

1 tablespoons of mixed herbs

½ tablespoons of red chili flakes

A small pinch of salt to taste

1 tablespoons of lemon juice

1 cup molten cheese

Directions:

Preheat the oven for 10 minutes at 200 Fahrenheit. What you need to do now is to boil the potatoes and blanch them. Combine all the ingredients for the marinade and add the potato fingers to it making sure that they are coated well. Place it in the oven and cook it at the same temperature for 25 minutes. In between the process, toss the fries twice or thrice so that they get cooked properly. Garnish with cheese and serve immediately.

Avocado Toast

Total time: 10 minutes

Prep time: 10 minutes

Cook time: 2 minutes

Yield: 4 servings

Ingredients:

2 ripe avocados, peeled

Squeeze of fresh lemon juice, to taste

2 tablespoons of fresh chopped mint, and extra to garnish

Sea salt and black pepper, to taste

5 large slices rye bread

85 grams soft feta, crumbled

Directions:

Take a medium bowl, and mash the avocado roughly with a fork; add lemon juice and mint and continue mashing until just combined. Season with black pepper as much as you like and sea salt to taste. Grill or toast bread until golden. Spread a part of the avocado mixture that you prepared onto each slice of the toasted bread and later top with feta. Garnish with extra mint and serve it soon.

Veggie Omelet

Total time: 40 minutes

Prep time: 15 minutes

Cook time: 25 minutes

Yield: 4 servings

Ingredients:

1 tablespoon. of extra virgin olive oil

2 cups of fennel bulb thinly sliced

¼ cup chopped artichoke hearts, soaked and drained

¼ cup pitted green olives

1 diced italian tomato

6 eggs

¼ tablespoon of sea salt

½ tsp. freshly ground black pepper

½ cup goat cheese, crumbled

2 tablespoon of freshly chopped fresh parsley, dill, or basil

Directions:

Preheat your oven to 325°F. Now heat extra virgin olive oil in an ovenproof skillet over medium heat for about 5 minutes until it will be tender. Add artichoke hearts, olives, and tomatoes and cook for 3 minutes or more (keep an eye while cooking). The important thing is that it must be softened. Take a big bowl, beat the eggs and then season with sea salt and pepper as you wish. After putting the egg mixture in the vegetables and stir for about a few minutes. Season the omelet with cheese and bake in the oven for about 5 minutes or until set and cooked through. Top with parsley, dill, or basil. Transfer the omelet onto a cutting board, carefully cut into four wedges, and serve until it's hot.

Week 3

Radish Flat cakes

Total time: 20 minutes

Prep time: 15 minutes

Cook time: 30minutes

Yield: 4 servings

Ingredients:

2 tablespoons of garam masala

2 cups sliced radish

3tablespoons of ginger finely chopped

1 few tablespoons of fresh coriander leaves

3 green chilies finely chopped

1 ½ tablespoons of lemon juice

Salt and pepper to taste

Directions:

Preheat the oven at 160 degrees Fahrenheit for 5 minutes. In the meanwhile mix carefully the ingredients in a clean bowl and add water to it, making sure that the paste is not too watery and is enough to apply on the radish. Place the galettes in the oven and let them cook for another 25 minutes at the same temperature. Continue rolling them over to get a uniform cook. Serve either with mint chutney or ketchup or with other sauces.

Summer salad served with Bacon and Brie Omelette

Total time: 15 minutes

Prep time: 5 minutes

Cook time: 10 minutes

Yield: 4 servings

Ingredients:

2tablespoons of olive oil

200g smoked lardons

5 or 6 eggs , lightly beaten

Small bunch chives, snipped

110 g of brie, sliced

1 tablespoons of red wine vinegar

1 tablespoons of mustard

1 cucumber, deseeded and sliced on the diagonal

250g radishes, quartered

Directions:

First at all, turn on the grill and heat 1 tablespoons of the oil in a small pan. Combine the lardons and fry until crisp and golden and then drain on kitchen paper. Take a non-stick frying pan and heat 2 tablespoons of the olive oil. Combine with the eggs, lardons, chives and some ground black pepper. Pour into the frying pan and cook over a low heat until semi-set, finally lay the brie on top. Grill until set and golden. After doing so remove from the pan and cut into wedges just before serving. You should also mix the remaining olive oil, vinegar, mustard and seasoning in a bowl; toss in the cucumber and radishes, and serve alongside the omelette wedges. Enjoy the meal!

Healthy Chopped Salad with Grilled Tofu

Total time: 45 minutes

Prep time: 30 minutes

Cook time: 15 minutes

Yield: 4 servings

Ingredients for Tofu:

1 tablespoon of extra virgin olive oil

¼ cup lemon juice

2 tablespoons of dried oregano

3 cloves garlic, minced

½ tablespoon of sea salt and ground pepper

14/15 ounces water-packed extra-firm tofu

Ingredients for salad:

2 tablespoon of extra virgin olive oil

¼ cup coarsely chopped Kalamata olives

¼ cup chopped scallions

1 cup diced seedless cucumber

2 medium tomatoes, diced

¼ cup chopped fresh parsley

1tablespoon of white-wine vinegar and ground pepper

Sea salt as much as you want

Directions:

Preheat your grill. Take a small bowl, add extra virgin olive oil, lemon juice, oregano, garlic, sea salt and black pepper; reserve two tablespoons of the mixture for basting. At this point, drain tofu and rinse, paying attention to pat dry with paper towels. Cut tofu crosswise into some thick slices and place in a glass dish. Put the lemon juice marinade and turn tofu in order to coat well. Let rest in the fridge for 30 minutes or even more. While waiting, go ahead preparing the salad. Take a medium bowl, and combine all the salad ingredients; toss gently to mix well. Set aside and then brush the grill rack with oil. When ready, drain the marinated tofu and discard the marinade. Grill tofu over medium heat, for about 5 minutes on each side basting frequently with lemon juice marinade. Top with the salad and serve your delicious grilled tofu warm.

Tomato Soup with Cannellini Bean and Barley

Total time: 30 minutes

Prep time: 10 minutes

Cook time: 20 minutes

Yield: 4 servings

Ingredients:

15 ounce of can of reduced-sodium beans that have been drained and rinsed could be substituted

1 tablespoon of extra-virgin olive oil

3 cloves garlic, minced

255 g tomato purée Kosher salt Freshly ground pepper

¼ cup freshly chopped parsley or basil

1 cup dried cannellini beans, covered in hot water overnight, and drained

710 ml Vegetable or Chicken Stock

½ cup pearl barley

¼ cup grated Italian Pecorino Romano cheese

Directions:

Initially, heat oil in a medium size saucepan over medium heat. Help yourself using garlic and sauté until its aroma will be released. It will take around 1 minute. After that, add tomato purée, salt, and pepper. Raise the heat to high and bring to a boil. You should then add parsley or basil and cannellini beans. Stir, reduce heat to low, and cover. Simmer for 15/20 minutes. Pay attention when you remove the lid. Stir in the stock and bring to a boil, uncovered, over high heat. At heat low, stir in the barley, and cook for about 15 minutes until the barley is well cooked (al dente). Garnish with cheese and serve hot.

Mushroom Tikka

Total time: 40 minutes

Prep time: 10 minutes

Cook time: 30 minutes

Yield: 4 servings

Ingredients:

1 onion cut it into quarters

5 tablespoons of gram flour

2 cups sliced mushrooms

1 big capsicum cut into big cubes

A pinch of salt to taste

For chutney:

2 tablespoons of ginger-garlic paste

1 small onion

2 cup fresh green coriander

½ cup mint leaves

4 tablespoons of fennel

6-7 flakes garlic (optional)

3 tablespoons of lemon juice

Salt to taste

Directions:

Take a container where you can mix together the fennel, coriander, onion/garlic, mint, and ginger, salt and lemon juice. After tahta, pour the mixture into a grinder and blend. You should get a thick paste. Next, slit the mushroom and leave them aside for the moment. At this point, stuff all the pieces with the paste and set aside. Add the chutney to the gram flour and add some salt before combining them together well. Rub this mixture all over the stuffed mushroom and add the capsicum and onions to the leftover chutney. After applying the chutney on each of the pieces of capsicum and onion, take satay sticks and arrange the cottage cheese pieces and vegetables on separate sticks. Preheat your oven at 290 Fahrenheit for 10 minutes and cook everything at 180 degrees for around half an hour remembering that the sticks with the vegetables just need to be cooked at the same temperature for only 7 or 8 minutes. During the cooking process, turn the sticks in between to get a uniform cook. Serve immediately.

Turkish Eggplant and Herbed Rice Pilaf

Total time: 15 minutes

Prep time: 5 minutes

Cook time: 10 minutes

Yield: 4 servings

Ingredients:

1 pound of eggplant, cut into 1-inch cubes

⅓ cup good-quality olive oil, divided

1 large onion, finely chopped

3 tablespoons pine nuts or blanched almonds

2 medium ripe tomatoes, peeled and chopped

1 teaspoon of unrefined sea salt or salt ground black pepper

1 teaspoon pure cinnamon

½ teaspoon allspice

2 tablespoons chopped fresh parsley

2 tablespoons of chopped fresh dill

1½ cups of Vegetable or Chicken Stock

Water as much as necessary

White basmati rice, soaked (for 20 minutes) and drained

Directions:

Preheat the broiler before starting. Place the eggplant on a baking sheet lined with aluminum foil. Next, pour ¼ cup of olive oil over the top and mix well to coat. Place the eggplant under the broiler and now broil until it will become light golden. It will take you around 3 or 5 minutes, be careful not to burn it. Remove from the oven and set aside. Combine the remaining olive oil to a large saucepan with a fitting lid. Don't forget to put the onion and sauté 3 to 5 minutes, until translucent. Stir in the nuts and sauté just until they change color. Mix the tomatoes, salt, pepper, cinnamon, allspice, parsley, dill, and reserved eggplant. Boil the water and put the rice into the mixture and stir. At this point, reduce heat to low. Put two paper towels on the top of the saucepan and cover it. After doing so, simmer for 25 to 30 minutes, pay attention that the rice will be tender and stock has been absorbed. Try to taste, adjust seasonings if necessary, and transfer to a heated serving platter.

Griddled chicken in quinoa Greek salad

Total time: 20 minutes

Prep time: 10 minutes

Cook time: 10 minutes

Yield: 4 servings

Ingredients:

225g quinoa

25 g of butter

1 red chilli deseeded and finely chopped

1 garlic clove crushed

400g chicken mini fillets

1½ tablespoon extra-virgin olive oil

300g vine tomato roughly chopped

A handful pitted black Kalamata olive

1 red onion finely sliced

100g crumbled feta cheese

small bunch of mint leaves

juice and zest

½ lemon or more

Directions:

After preparing the quinoa as written in the pack instructions, rinse in cold water and drain thoroughly. In the meanwhile, mix the butter, chilli and garlic into a paste. Now it is the time to toss the chicken fillets in 2 tablespoons of the olive oil with some seasoning. After that, put it in a hot griddle pan and cook for a few minutes each side. Next, transfer to a plate, dot with the spicy butter and set aside to melt; and combine the tomatoes, olives, onion, feta and mint into a bowl with the cooked quinoa. Stir through the remaining olive oil, lemon juice and zest, and don't forget to season well. You can serve with the chicken fillets on top, in alternative with any other chicken juices.

Week 4

Kashi Salad

Total time: 1 hour 35 minutes

Prep time: 15 minutes

Cook time: 1 hour

Cooling time: 20 minutes

Yield: 4 servings

Ingredients:

4 tablespoon of extra virgin olive oil

1 small onion, finely chopped

Small quantity of sea salt

Freshly ground black pepper, to taste

2 cups water

1 cup Kashi

7 Grain Pilaf

2 bay leaves

½ tablespoons of fresh lemon juice

5 tablespoons of sliced natural almonds, divided

8 cherry tomatoes, quartered

¼ cup chopped parsley

Chopped fresh mint (¼ cup)

4 large romaine leaves

Directions:

Prepare to heat 2 tablespoons of extra virgin olive oil in a large saucepan set over medium heat. Here try to add onion, sea salt and pepper and cook, stirring occasionally, for about 5 minutes or until lightly browned and tender. After that, stir in 2 cups of water, Kashi, bay leaves, sea salt and pepper; bring the mixture to a rolling boil, lower heat to a simmer and cook. Let it cover for about 40 minutes so the Kashi will be tender. Next, transfer to a large bowl and discard bay leaves. You should then stir in the remaining extra virgin olive oil, and lemon juice. At least 20 minutes it's important to let it sit until cooled or. Adjust the seasoning if desired without adding to much salt, and also 4 tablespoons of almonds, tomatoes, parsley, and mint. Mix everything and place one romaine leaf on each of the four plates and spoon the mixture into the center of the leaves. Use extra virgin olive oil and sprinkle with the remaining almonds. Enjoy your meal!

Egg Veggie

Scramble Total time: 30 minutes

Prep time 15 minutes

Cook time 15 minutes

Yield: 2 servings

Ingredients:

2 tablespoons of extra virgin olive oil, divided

1 medium orange bell pepper, diced

½ cup frozen corn kernels

1 scallion, thinly sliced

¼ tsp. cumin, freshly ground

¼ tsp. allspice, plus a pinch

2 eggs 2 egg whites Pinch of cinnamon

⅓ cup white cheddar, shredded

1 medium avocado, diced

½ cup fresh salsa

2 whole-wheat flour tortillas, warmed

Directions:

First of all, heat a teaspoon of olive oil in a nonstick pan over medium heat and then add bell pepper, tossing and turning for 5 minutes until soft; add the corn, scallion, cumin, and allspice and cook for a further few minutes until the scallion wilts. Pour everything in a plate and cover it with foil. Wipe the pan clean with a paper towel and set it aside. Place the eggs and egg whites in a bowl and whisk them with energy. Add water, a pinch of allspice and a pinch of cinnamon. Now it's time to heat the remaining olive oil in the pan. It's important that it is made with medium heat. Don't forget to add up the egg mixture. Cook until the bottom sets, for some seconds, then stir gently. Continue stirring for about 3 minutes or more, and then add the shredded cheese and vegetables that you had wrapped in foil. Serve the tortillas with avocado and salsa.

Strawberry Smoothie

Total time: 10 minutes

Prep time: 5 minutes

Cook time 5 minutes

Yield: 2 servings

Ingredients:

1 overripe banana, sliced

1 cup (100 g) ice

1 cup (230 g) yogurt

2 tablespoons (40 g) organic honey,

or to taste

1 cup (145 g) strawberries

2 tablespoons (24 g) flaxseeds

Directions:

First, blend the banana with ice, yogurt, and honey together. Next, add the strawberries and flaxseeds and blend on low speed for 30 seconds or until frothy. Serve cold with a clear glasses.

Mediterranean Tradition

Traditionally, many facial and skin care regimens in the Mediterranean regions utilized fruits as their primary ingredients. Try combining yogurt with honey and applying it over dry skin. Leave on for 20 minutes, rinse, and dry. Your skin will be benefit by it. The best result is undoubtedly softness.

Mediterranean Pancakes

Total time: 50 minutes

Prep time: 30 minutes

Cook time: 20 minutes

Yield: 16 Pancakes

Ingredients:

1 cup old-fashioned oats

½ cup all-purpose flour

2 tablespoons of flax seeds

1 tablespoon of baking soda

¼ tablespoon of sea salt

2 tablespoons of extra virgin olive oil

2 large eggs

2 cups nonfat plain Greek yogurt

2 tablespoons of raw honey

Fresh fruit, syrup, or other toppings

Directions:

In a blender, combine oats, flour, flax seeds, baking soda, and sea salt; blend for some seconds. After that proceed adding extra virgin olive oil, eggs, yogurt, and honey and continue pulsing until very smooth. In doing so, you allow the mixture to become thick. It will take around 20 minutes. At this point, set a large nonstick skillet over medium heat and brush with extra virgin olive oil. In batches, ladle the batter gently by quarter-cupfuls into the set. The time for cooking the pancakes is about 2 minutes or until bubbles form and golden brown. Turn them over and cook the other sides for 3 minutes or more until golden brown. At the end, place the cooked pancakes to a baking sheet and keep them warm in the oven. Serve with favorite toppings and eat immediately.

Mediterranean Barley Salad

Total time: 1 hour 45 minutes

Prep time: 15 minutes

Cook time: 30 minutes

Chilling time: 1 hour

Yield: 6 servings

Ingredients:

Water as much as necessary (around 2 ½ cups)

1 cup barley

4 tablespoons of extra virgin olive oil

2 cloves garlic

7 sun-dried tomatoes

1 tablespoon of balsamic vinegar

½ cup chopped black olives

½ cup finely chopped cilantro

Directions:

Starting with mixing water and barley in a saucepan; bring the mixture to a rolling boil over high heat. Once you the heat is lower to medium-low, simmer and cover it for about 30 minutes or until tender, but maintain a bit firm in the center. Drain and transfer to a large bowl; wait until the cooked barley reaches the room temperature. In a blender, mix 2 tablespoons of extra virgin olive oil with garlic, sun-dried tomatoes, and balsamic vinegar until very smooth; after that pour over barley and fold in the remaining olive oil, olives, and cilantro. Leave in the refrigerator until chilled. Pay attention to stir to mix well before serving.

Pasta with Broccoli and Garlic

Total time: 20minutes

Prep time: 10 minutes

Cook time: 10minutes

Yield: 6 servings

Ingredients:

1/3 cup of cold pressed olive oil, preferably Puglian

3 cloves garlic, finely chopped

½ minced chile pepper or ½ teaspoon red chili flakes

¼ cup pine nuts

12 small cherry tomatoes, quartered

½ teaspoon unrefined sea salt or salt

¼ teaspoon fresh-ground black pepper

½ pound broccoli florets

Italian parsley or 2 tablespoons of chopped basil

1 pound of whole-wheat pasta (orecchiette would be preferable. In alternative any short rice pasta)

¼ cup of grated Italian Pecorino Romano cheese

Directions:

Heat the olive oil in a large, wide skillet over medium heat and then gently add the garlic and chile pepper and sauté for 1 or 2 minute, just until they smell good. Combine the pine nuts and sauté until lightly golden without forgetting about the cherry tomatoes, salt, and pepper. Stir, and cook for 2 minutes. Later, add the broccoli florets, basil or parsley, and the necessary water, stir, and cover. Cook until the broccoli is fork-tender. In the meanwhile cook the pasta in a large pot of slightly salted boiling water for about 11/12 minutes, or until al dente so ready to be eaten. Drain, and put the finished sauce in it before adjusting or seasonings, if necessary. Top with Italian Pecorino Romano cheese or other cheese.

Rose and Mint Fruit Salad

Total time: 1 day

Prep time: 5 minutes

Yield: 4 servings

Ingredients:

1 cup of cubed cantaloupe

½ cup of raspberries

½ cup of strawberries

½ cup of blueberries

½ cup of sliced kiwi

Sugar (¼ cup or less)

1 teaspoon rose water

4 tablespoons of finely chopped fresh mint

4 teaspoons of yogurt, for garnish

Directions:

Combine all of the fruit in a large salad bowl with the sugar, rose water, and mint. Proceed drizzling the sugar mixture over fruit. At this point, cover the bowl, and store in the refrigerator from 6 hours to overnight. Transfer to individual bowls before serving. If desired Garnish with yogurt.

Bulgur Salad

Total time: 30 minutes

Prep time: 10 minutes

Cook time: 20 minutes

Yield: 4 servings

Ingredients:

1 tablespoon of unsalted butter

2 or 3 tablespoon extra virgin olive oil, divided

2 cups bulgur

Water as much as necessary

¼ tablespoon of sea salt

1 medium cucumber, deseeded and chopped

2 tablespoon red wine vinegar

¼ cup dill, chopped

1 handful black olives, pitted and chopped

Directions:

Place a saucepan over medium heat and add the butter and the olive oil. Toast the bulgur in the oil until it turns golden brown and starts to crackle. Add water to the saucepan and season with the salt (start with a small quantity of water). At this point, you have to cover the saucepan and simmer until all the water gets absorbed for about 20 minutes or even more. Before or after doing that, put in a mixing bowl, the chopped cucumber with dill, olives, red wine vinegar and the remaining olive oil. Serve this over the bulgur and enjoy it.

Mushroom Patties

Total time: 25 minutes

Prep time: 10 minutes

Cook time: 15 minutes

Yield: 6 servings

Ingredients:

1 cup of minced mushroom

A pinch of salt to taste

¼ tablespoons of ginger finely chopped

1 green chili finely chopped

1 tablespoon of lemon juice and one of a fresh coriander leaves

¼ tablespoon of red chili powder

¼ tsp. cumin powder

Directions:

Combine all the ingredients mentioned above and make sure that the flavors are right. At this point, make round patties with the mixture and roll them out in a good way. Preheat your oven (or your air fryer) at 250 Fahrenheit for 5 minutes.Lower the heat at 150 degrees for around 10 or 12 minutes. In between the cooking process, don't forget to turn the patties over to get a uniform cook. Serve hot with mint chutney.

Conclusion

The Mediterranean diet is definitely one of the keys to the fountain of youth. The main reason why it is so powerful is because it contains a lot of fresh, natural, rich nutritious, and it's in general a wholesome healthy food profile. If you try this diet you will start noticing distinct improvements in your appearance as well as energy levels as soon as you start. The Mediterranean diet allows you to eat various foods for better health later.

Made in United States
North Haven, CT
21 May 2022

19416718R00095